NEVER GROW UP

Christian Blond

NEVER GROW UP

HOW TO BE HAPPY AND FULFILL YOUR DREAMS?

© Blond Books / Blond Finance OÜ, 2015
WWW.BLONDBOOKS.COM

Illustrated by Leo Lätti
Edited by Külli Kuusk
Layout by Angelika Schneider

ISBN 978-9949-38-211-8
Printed by Tallinn Book Printers

*To my dear and delightfully
childlike wife Jaanika,
who encouraged me to write this book.*

Contents

Foreword

What distinguishes happy people from unhappy ones? How come some fulfill their dreams with no effort, and some never make their dreams come true? Two people may do exactly the same things side by side, and yet, one is happy and the other isn't. One of them fulfills their dreams. However, the other doesn't even come close. Even though the one that is happy and successful isn't necessarily smarter, better educated, better looking or in any way better than the other one. The answer is that the only thing that separates the happy from the unhappy is their ATTITUDE.

All of us have seen how our attitudes can vary. Sometimes we are on top of everything. We are driven by this special enthusiasm that makes everything we do go smoothly. You are in a good mood, and you are open, creative, cheerful, joyful and bright at the same time. You feel present in the moment and participate in life whole-heartedly.

At other times, it seems that you are surrounded by a cloud of negative attitude – everything goes wrong, we are tuned to a wrong wavelength. We tend to overcomplicate things, we are in a bad mood, have a hostile attitude, and are pessimistic. We can't enjoy the moment to the full, and we are kind of distracted and disturbed.

Many self-motivation books talk about how to tune in to the right wavelength and move towards the fulfillment of our dreams. Why write another book, then? Because I feel that many happy-living books say the right stuff, but many of them overcomplicate things – having read some of them, we may agree with what we have found out, but we are in more confusion than before picking up the book.

A good advice or a good theory is always short, not long, because we won't remember the most important and main message from a long and vague theory. This book tells you how to be happy in just three words: "Never grow up". The book will thoroughly explain this idea, so that you would fully understand this easy and memorable message. Each chapter discusses a specific difference between a childlike and an adult attitude, and at the end of each chapter, there is a story about a person that has changed world history with their childlike attitude, such as Robert De Niro, Abraham Lincoln, Leonardo da Vinci, Oprah, John Lennon, and Steve Jobs.

Throughout my entire conscious life, I have studied the differences between happy and unhappy people. Let me assure you with absolute conviction that attitude is the only thing that makes us either happy or unhappy. And that's a good thing, because it means that it's within our power to increase our level of happiness and improve our quality of life. All happy people either consciously or unconsciously use a childlike attitude.

There are 40 examples of world-famous people from different walks of life, who have fulfilled their dreams namely thanks to their childlike attitude. Therefore, it's absolutely certain that this attitude can also help you to fulfill your dreams, whatever your profession or whatever your dreams may be! Hopefully, reading this book will be an exciting experience and leave you enjoying your life (even) more than before.

Happy reading!

Introduction

The advice, "Never grow up" doesn't mean that you should behave like a child: stamp your feet, throw tantrums and play all day. No. The advice solely concerns your mental state, attitude towards life. This is because your attitude and mentality are the basic things that influence your life and determine, whether you can be happy and fulfill your dreams, or not.

Grown-ups have a lot that children don't yet possess. Grown-ups are more experienced, wiser, better-educated, their abilities are bigger in all respects. Children are still developing in that direction. But despite the fact that grown-ups are so much more capable than children, they aren't necessarily happier than children are.

Even the same person may not be happier as a grown-up than as a child. They might of course be happier as an adult, but they may also be much less satisfied with their life. It seems like a paradox that grown-ups that are so perfect and superior compared to children, are still unable to be happy. It should be a child's play to wise and developed people like us. But it isn't.

The fact that prevents us from enjoying life and striving towards our perfect potential is the same adult wisdom, knowledge and maturity. Everything that grown-ups have better than kids, works against us. Our rational attitude won't let us enjoy life and reach for the fulfillment of our dreams with all our might.

When an adult wakes up in a beautiful spring morning, they may not even notice the beauty of that morning. There are so many responsibilities, tasks and problems to think about. And they have already seen their share of beautiful mornings.

But when a child wakes up on a beautiful spring morning, they only think about what a beautiful way it is to start the morning and what exciting things could be done in this lovely weather. They only focus on the moment and a single activity.

This book talks about how we can put aside all our experience and knowledge, and live only in the present moment – here and now – and fully enjoy our activities. With a childlike attitude, we are more effective at work, and at the same time, enjoy our activities much more.

With a childlike attitude, we move towards our dreams with playful ease, achieving results we didn't believe were possible, and feel no anguish or excessive strain. It is pretty much a walk in the park for us.

How is it possible? How can it be that sometimes, even despite the struggle, despite being unhappy throughout our efforts, we still only achieve mediocre results? In other cases, meanwhile, we work creatively, playfully and enjoying the moment wholeheartedly, yet achieve brilliant results while doing so.

The answer lies in the 40 stories in this book. They speak of the childlike attitude of outstanding people. Their childlike attitudes helped Elvis Presley become world-famous, Neil Armstrong to fly on the moon, Abraham Lincoln to save America, Rafael Nadal to play tennis, and Picasso to paint. This attitude is also certain to help you, whatever your wishes and dreams may be.

GROWN-UPS LIVE EVERYWHERE, CHILDREN ONLY IN THE MOMENT

Let me tell you an important secret that is beyond most grown-ups: life only happens in the present moment. The past has gone by already and the future has not yet arrived. Grown-ups tend to live either dwelling on past events, or planning the future. In this way, however, you can never enjoy the moment or live to the fullest. If you don't live to the fullest, you cannot be fully happy or successful.

Children, on the other hand, live in the present moment. They don't spend their time constantly planning their future or analyzing what has happened in the past. It seems as if adults have exchanged living their lives for analyzing them. The result might be that while grown-ups are busy making plans, life just passes them by.

Just like dwelling on the past, predicting the future is both thankless and futile. You can never foresee all the twists and turns of life and plan the things to come. The variability and unpredictability life has to offer will always undo any plans you may have. Children possess the skill of living in the moment. They play as if there was no tomorrow and concentrate on what is going on right here, right now.

You should also learn from the kids and live in the present moment only. Imagine a child playing with their toys. They aren't distracted by anything else. They are fully engaged in what they are doing. They don't feel guilty for failing in previous games. They also don't try to predict what they will be playing the next day or the day after that. They fully focus only on the game they are playing at that moment. Adults who are successful in their field practice the same thing. The secret of every successful person is complete devotion to what they do namely in the present moment. This is the only way of solving the tasks before us to a high standard.

It often happens that idleness is your best choice. Grown-ups try to do everything at once, quickly and efficiently. When an adult is drinking morning coffee, they are already driving to work in their mind. When they have sat in the car, they are already planning their lunch break. Rushing along this way, we fail to notice the right solutions that can be noticed only when living in the moment and taking time for being idle.

When you spend time doing absolutely nothing, you switch off the so-called cerebral auto-pilot and your mind can start working more effectively. This enables you to see your problems from a new angle, your creativity activates, and you can come up with innovative solutions that you hadn't noticed before due to hurrying.

A successful, child-minded businessman was once asked what he would recommend to the youngsters in the audience wishing to become as successful as he was. Or what would he recommend to older people thinking about becoming an entrepreneur. The successful businessman thought for a second and said that he had only one piece of advice: "Just get started!" The journalist asked clarifying questions about preparing for different projects, what to study or where to go, but the businessman held his ground and gave

the same answer: "Just get started straight away!" He explained that too much reasoning, research, preparation and so on shifts your focus off the main thing and doesn't allow you to concentrate on getting started.

The most important thing is to get down to business, for the world is full of magnificent but unrealized plans and good intentions. I get his advice perfectly! The hardest part of every journey is always the first step of getting started.

Grown-ups constantly postpone their plans, but the right moment never arrives. All you need to do is to just live in the moment like a child, and be brave, fearless like a child, and get started right away! Planning, contemplating, thinking – these are truly adult and wise things to do, but they are also the opposite to real action. If you begin right away and start from the beginning, you will have plenty of time to do planning, contemplating and thinking along the way. You can always make plans, but you cannot miss the right moment of getting started!

You don't need to know where your journey ends, only where it begins. Just go ahead and when you get there, you'll discover new ways for going forward. Without embarking on a journey, you will never know where you could have ended up.

Any person successful in their field devotes themselves to completely what they are doing that exact moment, just like a child focuses only on what they are doing in the present moment.

A STORY OF LIVING IN THE PRESENT MOMENT LIKE A CHILD

—

Rihanna

Millions of little girls around the world dream of becoming a world-famous superstar. Sometimes, the parents are the ones that try to direct their child on that golden path. They hire an expensive tutor, the child is sent to study at a music school with a reputable history, take dancing lessons and listen to motivational lectures.

Rihanna's example is different. She was born in 1988 on the small and gorgeous Caribbean island of Barbados. Robyn Rihanna was the eldest of three children in the family. Her father worked as a storekeeper and her mother as an accountant. Her childhood curiously gave her the first lessons in doing business that she could use later in the tough music industry. She helped her father sell clothes on the street market. This definitely educated her in trade and the ins and outs of the market.

The business-minded Robyn invented another way to up her allowance. She would buy candy in bulk, wrap it in nice packages and sell it to other kids at school for a profit. Robyn Rihanna's childhood was strongly influenced by her father's alcohol and drug addiction and her parents' quarrelsome marriage that ended when Rihanna was 14.

Rihanna loved singing to herself at home since when she was little. It was nothing out of the ordinary, considering the culture of Barbados. She was an introverted child and music was her way of expressing herself. She was singing all the time – to her relatives, teddy bears, even her pillows – and dreamt of becoming a star one day.

Although her vocal abilities emerged in the early childhood, she found no wider audience to her singing in the first fifteen years of her life. She could do music only for her own pleasure or sometimes perform with her friends at school. After her parents got divorced, the shy teenage girl started practicing singing more and more just to get away from the problems at home. At the age of 15, she established a three-member girl group with her classmates.

It happened one time that Evan Rogers, a music producer from New York, was spending his holiday on the island. Since Rogers' wife Jackie is from Barbados, he visits the island quite often. "I'm always there, and people know I'm a record producer and a songwriter, so everyone knows someone who wants to audition for me," he says. This is exactly what happened then, in 2004.

Rihanna's and her friends' audition was arranged through mutual acquaintances. "One of them was Robyn Fenty, and she stood out," Rogers recalls the life-changing meeting. "She had this incredible presence when she walked in." Music producer Evan Rogers asked Rihanna to return the next day without her friends and invited her and her mother to go and live with him in Stamford, America, with the intention of making her a star.

In spite of Rihanna's pleas, her mother was against it at first. Rihanna's mother relented only later when she found out that Evan's wife was from Barbados. In less than a year, the then only 16-year-old Rihanna moved in with Evan Rogers and his wife in Connecticut and started working on a demo album.

"I'M REALLY LOOKING FORWARD
TO SEEING WHAT LIFE BRINGS
TO ME."

–

Robyn Rihanna Fenty

"When I left Barbados, I didn't look back," says Rihanna. "I wanted to do what I had to do, even if it meant moving to America." Evan and Jackie became something of a second family for the shy Rihanna. With his business partner Carl Sturken, Evan recorded Rihanna's first demo and the rest is history – Rihanna became an international R&B superstar.

When Rihanna was still a humble girl from the small and poor island of Barbados, she didn't focus on how bad her domestic life was but eagerly looked for things she could do. She also never made big plans or spent her time on dreaming or planning. She lived in the moment like a child and concentrated on singing. She didn't sing because someone suggested she should do it or to achieve something no matter what. She mainly sang because she enjoyed it more than anything else in the world.

In her own words: "When you realize who you live for, and who's important to please, a lot of people will actually start living. I am never going to get caught up in that. I'm gonna look back on my life and say that I enjoyed it – and I lived it for me."

GROWN-UPS WORK, CHILDREN PLAY

Grown-ups believe that working long and hard leads them to achieving their goals. The reality is quite the opposite. Instead, you should focus on thoroughly enjoying your work, just as a child enjoys playing. Without exception, the formula of the success of all successful people is that they enjoy what they do. If a person worked 14 hours a day for 10 years in a row, they would still not achieve any success what so ever if they had no interest in the field. This has been illustrated by many examples from real life.

Look around yourself. Everywhere you look, you see people that are mediocre, unhappy and unsatisfied with their work. They will achieve no success! They just do their work – without passion, indifferently, numbly. They have never made an effort to think what kind of work they would really like to do.

The secret to success is not working longer and harder. The key is in spending your time and energy on searching for what you really like. You should pick a job the same way a child picks up activities – they never play a boring game, they only want to play something exciting!

Once you have found such an activity, you will no longer have to work for another day. Instead, you can start playing like a child. The best part of the bargain is that the work you are really good at, that you are deeply interested in and that you enjoy is where you will achieve the most remarkable results! To the best of your ability, that is. Because, don't forget that all of us won't become world-famous inventors, geniuses or pop stars. We have to play with the cards we were dealt at birth.

I don't want you to restrict yourself needlessly by aiming too high or too low. Neither option is good. Aiming too high can cause frustration and aiming too low will result in boredom. The healthiest and most productive way is to let life carry you, just like children trust the present moment. And then you must take the maximum out of it. Let's spend each moment playing the work that we like!

As grown-ups, our thinking gets stuck in certain patterns. At some point in our lives, there comes a moment when we wisely and soberly consider what profession would be respectable enough, we follow the most popular world trends etc. Grown-ups are interested in the respect of the community. Surely, there are different traditions around the world, but wise career choices are usually considered to include professions like business manager, doctor, lawyer etc. But this is only the society's expectation. If you want the community to really appreciate you, be yourself! Find an activity that absorbs you completely, even if it's contrary to the current trends.

If you feel real passion for your work, you can become a trend-setter yourself. You will receive the most recognition only when you find work that is as exciting to you as play is to a child. Of course, your work must benefit people or companies, because otherwise you won't get paid. Two things go hand in hand in this picture – demand for your work and the pay you get for it. So, the more you play and the better you do it, the more you will get paid. You spend most of your waking time at work. You cannot afford a situation where you have a job that you do not really like. This means that most of your life is nothing but unhappy! That would be simply unacceptable and sad!

Do you remember the moments in your childhood when you were in the middle of an exciting game? In that moment, life was so exciting that even going to the toilet seemed like a waste of time and you would have postponed it as long as you could. The urge to go was pretty big, but still you tried to hold it back.

When you're a grown-up and feel that you should rush back to work as fast as you can because you were in the middle of something interesting and exciting while sitting on the toilet, this is exactly the job for you. When you have never felt such excitement, you should think about whether the work you are doing is the right one for you. I advise you to search and never stop, until you have found a job just like that. Life is a game, play it!

*Grown-ups think that work is a forced
activity that you must tolerate.
Happy and successful people do not work for
even a day in their lives because their work
is like a game – they work with abandon,
passion and all their heart.*

A STORY ABOUT PLAYING LIKE A CHILD

—

Thomas A. Edison

To be exact, this is a story about Thomas A. Edison's parents. When the young Edison was only seven years old, his parents noticed that the boy was very special and talented. Thomas liked to question all grown-ups that he would meet about the origin of various phenomena. He also loved reading a lot. Meanwhile, his teacher G. B. Engle found him to be thick, because the boy didn't like maths and he asked too many questions. Back then, students were not allowed to ask questions. After three months at school, the teacher called Thomas addled, after which Thomas' mother Nancy Edison went to school to speak to the teacher. The teacher explained that Thomas was not concentrating and wasn't able to learn.

Fortunately, the boy Edison's parents had a childlike attitude. After hearing what the teacher had to say, Thomas's mother Nancy decided that she would home-school her son from there on. The boy had only been going to school for three months by that time. The parents were very dedicated to developing him. They didn't force him to study things he didn't enjoy. This way, the boy Edison could focus on what really interested him.

"I NEVER DID
A DAY'S WORK
IN MY LIFE.
IT WAS ALL FUN."
–
Thomas Alva Edison

Soon, he started to take more and more interest in chemistry and was always conducting all sorts of exciting chemical experiments. At the age of ten, Thomas built his first laboratory, located in the Edisons' cellar. Edison thoroughly enjoyed being home-schooled, because he didn't have to deal with tedious maths. However, hadn't Thomas' parents had such a childlike attitude, Thomas A. Edison would never have become a world-famous inventor. Had they acted like other parents, as befits a grown-up, the boy Edison would have carried on as a giftless below-average student who would have had to focus on getting through school before anything.

His mother made a brave and childlike decision by starting to home-school her talented son herself, encouraging him to constantly engage only in things that interested the boy the most. Thanks to his parents, the genius Thomas Alva Edison started to see his work as a game. By playing like a child, he could focus on developing his strengths and later created inventions that have changed everyone's lives of everyone. Who knows, maybe we would still be sitting in the dark if it weren't for his childishness.

ADULT LIFE IS HARD, CHILDREN'S LIFE IS EASY

From time to time, adults tend to get stuck in a deadlock, where life seems hard and there is no way out. Our minds work against us in situations where we are in up to our necks in a problem. Muddling in all of it, we cannot put the situation in perspective. For example, it's quite usual that a person with a relatively trivial problem blows it up in their mind to such proportions that they start using expressions like "my life is pointless", "my life is ruined" or "there is no way out", etc. Meanwhile, other people's difficulties can look silly to bystanders, because they can see the solutions. For example, you cannot say that your life is ruined or that it's pointless if the issue is only a late mortgage payment, a venomous comment from the boss or suchlike. These are all minor problems that mean nothing in the longer run.

Children, however, don't carry such burdens along. True, children have their small issues, but when going to the kindergarten on the following day, things will be sorted out. Kids don't get stuck in negative thought patterns for days and months on end, because their attitude is simpler and more pragmatic. Inexperience works in their favor. Kids think in a more intuitive and impulsive way. They let life carry them along. This is exactly what you should do as an adult.

The grown-up mind has a large capacity for analysis. The past is also full of negative experiences that in turn produce bad thought patterns. Grown-ups are scared and afraid that life will deal them new blows. You should keep an open mind towards life and harbor no prejudices, just as a child. Because the truth is that life is easy and every new day may offer several unexpected positive opportunities to us. Our own attitude needs to be anticipating and positive, just like that of a child, so we could use the future opportunities in the best possible way.

Life is easy, when we take the stance that life is easy. When we read about a success story from a magazine, we get the feeling as if achieving something big was like taking a walk from one victory to the next. But we are not shown the thousands of unsuccessful attempts at success. There is an illusion that achieving something big depends on a number of lucky breaks that have fallen in the lap of a lucky person for some unknown reason. But how do you explain the fact that the same people attract success repeatedly throughout their lives?

Of course, there is hard work and not giving up behind every kind of success. But the thing that inspires you not to give up is sincere hope and belief in the fulfilment of your goals. People tend to attract "lucky breaks" because they don't follow the adult mindset.

They do not have the attitude that life is hard – their motto is "life is easy". Maybe they believe in success in advance and that belief helps them attract lucky breaks. As they say, "Luck is what happens when preparation meets opportunity". Luck favors people who take the initiative. This kind of an open, hopeful and positive attitude, however, is totally childish. Adults just think and analyze, based on their wisdom and experience.

Wisdom questions the possibility of success. At the same time, belief is totally childish and doesn't stand to reason. Hope and belief are totally intuitive and spiritual attributes. You can only wholly hope and believe when you exchange your adult attitude for that of a child.

The childishness of our attitude determines how easy our life is. Sincere hope and belief is natural to children and the childish, not to adults.

A STORY ABOUT A CHILDISHLY EASY ATTITUDE TOWARDS LIFE
—
Oprah Winfrey

Oprah's childhood was one of poverty and hardship. The sufferings included sexual abuse that started at the age of 9, and giving birth to a child at the age of 14, when Oprah had a son that died as an infant. In spite of her extremely difficult childhood, Oprah quickly worked her way up, and at the age of 22, she became the co-anchor of the six O'clock news show on WJZ TV in Baltimore. That seemed like the peak of her career and fulfillment of her dreams. But unexpectedly, Oprah's career collapsed.

WJZ felt that Oprah looked detached and stiff on air and they noticed that she often mispronounced words. They fired her. Years later, Oprah recounted this moment in one of her shows: "At the time, I was devastated, devastated!" At that moment, Oprah could have given up, if she had followed the adult attitude that life is hard. But Oprah's attitude was childlike – she took life easily and was prepared to give it another go.

Instead of letting her go completely, WJZ looked for other opportunities for Oprah. Their talk show, *People are Talking*, was in bad shape and the channel owners had nothing to lose when they

"WHERE THERE IS NO STRUGGLE, THERE IS NO STRENGTH."
–
Orpah Gail Winfrey

made Oprah host the show. Oprah clutched at the straw and gave it her best. She blossomed as the host of the show. She had never had the opportunity to be herself when working as a news anchor. What initially seemed like the end of her career was actually the best thing that could have happened to her, because now she found her true calling. She could talk to people, approaching them in the personal and soulful manner that has remained the trademark of Oprah's shows to this day.

The TV show became a hit and the rest is history. According to the Forbes magazine, Oprah is the most influential celebrity in the world, and the richest self-made woman in America. Oprah childishly believed that life was easy and didn't give up despite all the difficulties, carrying on towards the fulfilment of her dreams. By the way, here's another good example of Oprah's childlike attitude: Oprah's real name was actually Orpah, but since her family and people around her kept calling her Oprah, she adopted the more palatable version. A fun and childlike decision in my book.

GROWN-UPS FIND THEMSELVES IMPORTANT, CHILDREN DON'T

It often happens that the more insignificant adults are in their work and activities, the more they wish to make themselves important. They try to leave an impression of their own importance and the unimportance of others. For example, they can seek fame and attention at all costs. Instead, let's follow the example of someone who everybody respects and who has achieved something in their life. Such a personality may emphasize the importance of their work or some other activity, but never their own person. Distinguished and important people have a simple and childlike attitude towards themselves.

Be careful around people that take themselves too seriously. They will try to throw spanners in the works of others at every opportunity, being in the state of some constant competition and negative race and comparison. But a person that always criticizes others is never happy themselves, because this constant competing and self-promotion creates negativity. It also means they can never achieve real success, because success comes only with the help of others. When thinking more of ourselves than others and not appreciating others, we cut off the opportunity to use other people's help. This way, we are left alone with our goals and desires and won't get very far.

There is only one way to become someone really important – when other people start considering us important. Children don't regard themselves important. They have not yet developed intellectually to the point where they are able to give such significance to their own person. Children's attention is focused on their surrounding environment and their activities. Excessive self-importance remains only the domain of adults.

If we wish to be happy as grown-ups and make something really happen in our lives, we should only focus on sensing our surround-

ings and on our activity. We should leave aside any kind of self-promotion, as that will only give other people warning signals – they will regard us as a whippersnapper or an upstart. Adults that consider themselves important may pretend to be happy, but on the inside, they are always restless and unhappy. Their unfortunate destinies also testify to that fact. It seems as if a constant shadow of misfortune has followed them around. However, the misfortune is attracted by their own negativity and self-importance.

Have as little to do as possible with people that unduly and in an adult way regard themselves too important. If you wish to live happily and in harmony, you need to keep yourself as pure and simple as a child as possible. Your attitude towards your own person

should be playful, like a child's. Concentrating on your present activity and the surroundings makes it a piece of cake to feel happy and do remarkable things. You will feel as if you were one with others and the environment, just as children do.

If you can distance yourself from your personality and focus on the surrounding world, you will seem to live in a higher realm of consciousness where you feel absolutely complete and one with the surrounding world. Your senses are sharp, your mind is fresh, and you have a fun, childlike attitude. This state of mind is always out of the reach of intellectuals that think they're important.

Adults love feeling important about themselves. However, we can ever become really important only when others consider us important. Children focus on their activity and the surrounding environment. If you wish to be happy, focus only on your activity and the surroundings, abstaining from self-importance. This way, you will ascend from your personal level to the heights where it is simple to achieve and be happy.

A STORY ABOUT CHILDLIKE LACK
OF SELF-IMPORTANCE
—
Cristiano Ronaldo

Cristiano Ronaldo is one of the best and highest-earning soccer players of all time. When talking about childlike lack of self-importance, Ronaldo doesn't seem like a good example at first sight, as many regard him to be a selfish player and a vain pretty boy. But the external image or first impression doesn't necessarily reflect his true nature.

In the recent 2014 Champions League Final, Ronaldo's team Real Madrid defeated another Spanish club, Atletico Madrid, in overtime with the score 4:1. For Real Madrid, it was the tenth title in the club's history, the last one coming 12 years earlier. When celebrating the victory after the game, for the amazement of the thousands of spectators gathered in the Lisbon stadium and the millions of people watching it on TV, Ronaldo abandoned his team-mates and ran to the stands, pulling out a man from the crowd and embracing him affectionately.

This symbolic act was both a public confession and a tribute to Albert Fantrau, his childhood friend and training partner to whom Ronaldo allegedly owes his success.

The story itself took place long before Ronaldo became the star of Manchester United, the captain of the Portuguese national team and a global icon. Ronaldo and Albert were on the same team at the U-18 championships on their home island of Madeira. The boys were forced to compete against each other, however, when the talent hunter that had come to watch the game told them, "Whoever scores more goals will will be accepted at our academy".

Ronaldo has recounted this in an interview to the media: "We won that match 3-0. I scored the first goal and then Albert scored the second with a great header. But the third goal was impressive for all of us. Albert was one-on-one against the goalkeeper, he rounded the goalkeeper and I was running in front of him.

"All he had to do was to score that goal but he passed it to me and I scored the third goal, so I got that spot and went to the academy. "After the match I went to him and asked him why? Albert said that "Because you (Ronaldo) are better than me."

After the interview with Ronaldo, journalists went to Albert's house and asked him if the story was true. Albert Fantrau said it was. He also said that his career as a soccer player ended after that match and he became unemployed. A journalist asked, "But how did you build this house so great, you have a car? You seem like a rich man. You also able keep your family. From where did this come from?"

Albert answered with pride: "It is from Ronaldo!" Ronaldo may make cocky statements and leave a selfish impression, but dedicating one of the most significant victories of his career to his childhood friend shows that he has a childishly simple attitude towards himself and he doesn't regard himself too important in an adult way. This childlike attitude has enabled Ronaldo become a legendary soccer player.

"WITHOUT FOOTBALL, MY LIFE IS WORTH NOTHING."

–

Cristiano Ronaldo dos Santos Aveiro

GROWN-UPS ARE TIMID, CHILDREN ARE BRAVE

As a child, we sincerely believe that when we grow up, we'll become a conductor, pilot, astronaut, or maybe a famous singer or by chance even the president. Children have no fears, just like they have no real experiences. Grown-ups, on the other hand, have plenty of experience, but at some point in life many lose courage. But one should always keep their courage. We should hold on to the childish courage as grown-ups. If a person lacks courage, they lose a part of themselves – a part of their charisma and self-confidence.

What distinguishes happy people from the unhappy is the lack of courage. It's not possible to be a coward and a happy person at the same time. Being brave does not mean that we cannot have any fears. Quite the opposite. Being brave means that we act despite of fear. Children are brave, because they lack negative experiences. They are not held back by endless unsuccessful attempts and failures. If a child learns to walk, he will fall on all fours hundreds of times before he or she becomes steady on their feet. This kind of courage and will to develop is encoded in us.

As adults, we shouldn't start putting breaks on this will and courage with our minds, because then our development will stop and we won't achieve our goals. However, if we don't develop or move forward, we will surely never become happy. We must follow our inner drive to be brave, act despite our fear, take risks and continue to grow and learn. As grown-ups, we can only improve if we take risks, just as children do. We must act without knowing the outcome and hope for the best.

Every person shapes their own life. Adults that have given up living to the fullest, start making up excuses and explaining why their life has turned out the way it has. They find a thousand reasons why it wasn't their fault that their life ended up the way it did. It takes huge childlike courage to take responsibility for one's own fate.

Children don't think – they act. We must adopt the brave and decisive action of children. After some time, when we have acted in a brave and responsible way, we will see the results – our life will have changed for the better. If we behave like cowards, we will never be able to take such responsibility.

If you wished to become an astronaut as a child, reflect on why that was your dream. Was your desire to be a special and distinguished person? Did you dream of becoming a hero and drawing other people's admiration? Try to go back to your primal instincts and wishes. Think without fear what it is that you really want. The energy coming from your courage gives you strength and motivation to strive towards that goal. Just like children sincerely believe that they can become astronauts, you can become the superstar of your own life, someone that your loved ones or even a wider circle admires. Be a person that acts in a childlike and brave way. Don't be scared, go on bravely!

Children live bravely and freely. Failures hold grown-ups back. He who acts in a childlike way despite of fear is a brave person. Even brave people have their fears, but they go on in spite of the fear.

A STORY ABOUT CHILDLIKE COURAGE

—
Elvis Presley

Gladys, Elvis Presley's mother, remembers in one of her interviews how she took her son to a fair in their hometown, Tupelo. After hearing a guitar player perform, little Elvis told his mother, "I can sing better than him". Not to eat his words, he took to the stage right then and there, with his leg shaking a bit, and sang without any accompaniment. His mother said he sang in a powerful voice and he really was better than the guitarist that had just performed.

Years later, when Elvis was 19, he earned his living as a truck driver and still dreamt of a career as a singer, but he had no idea how to get started. The childlike courage, however, was still there. The competitive little brave boy who had wanted to make it as a singer more than anything was still alive inside him. The opportune moment came when his friend Ronnie Smith, already a member of a professional band, told Elvis that their soloist Eddie Bond was looking for a replacement while he was in the army.

Soon after that, Elvis appeared at the Hi Hat club, where he nervously performed some songs to Eddie Bond. But this time, things did not quite go like that time at the Tupelo fair as a little

"WHEN I WAS A BOY, I
ALWAYS SAW MYSELF
AS A HERO IN COMIC
BOOKS AND IN MOVIES.
I GREW UP BELIEVING
THIS DREAM."
–
Elvis Aaron Presley

boy. Bond turned him down, recommending him to remain a truck driver, "because you'll never make it as a singer".

In spite of this setback, Elvis bravely continued looking for his lucky break and a few months later, he recorded the single, "That's All Right (Mama)", that became a hit in Memphis and launched Elvis to world-wide fame. Yes, in order for a truck driver to become the king of rock 'n' roll, you need loads of childish courage – you need to bravely jump on the stage.

GROWN-UPS ARE KNOW-IT-ALLS, CHILDREN ARE SIMPLE

If a child wishes to know something, they ask about it in a loud and clear voice. Children aren't afraid to seem incompetent. They are not daunted by the fact that they don't know something that seems elementary in the adults' world. It's a part of being a child.

If a grown-up is incompetent at something, they don't dare to speak about it out loud. Yet, as adults, we wish to show others that we know everything about everything – like a real sidekick. A grown-up would instead just quietly find the answers themselves, rather than make a fool out of themselves in front of others.

When I take a cab or go to the barber's, I keep wondering how the barber or cab driver knows everything about everything. They may not necessarily be the wisest of all, but they somehow mastered the skill of coming across as a person that has answers to every single question. Knowing things "by their own wisdom", they may never be able to explain their thoughts fully. They never speak about what they really think. Instead, they just relay other people's opinions, usually widely common ones. In reality, it's often just empty chat leaving an impression of actually knowing something.

For example, in their own minds, they are completely competent to discuss and especially criticize top athletes. They themselves, however, have never done top-class sports. They know how to run the country, but they have never been engaged in politics themselves. In fact, their political views merely echo some recent political opinion piece. I believe I'm not the only one who, getting back from the airport or on my way back from a party on a Saturday night, has had to listen to the cab driver going on and on about politics or a better way of life. This is what typical grown-ups are like.

On the other hand, I am astonished by the simple and clear observations of a well-known scientist or a CEO of a major company, delivered in an inquisitive form and retaining a position of looking

for solutions instead of knowing everything. Professional attitude is characterized by the "I-don't-know-it-all" frame of mind, while people that are not top players in any walk of life think that their motto is "I know it all".

People laugh at grown-ups that are ignorant in some area. It is as if we were striving towards ultimate wisdom where mistakes and ignorance are not allowed. But this frame of mind stops us from living at our best. If you wish to be successful and happy and not have all the wonderful opportunities slip through your fingers, you must admit that are many things you don't yet know. You need to dare be as simple as a child. Only those who don't consider themselves omniscient can ask silly questions, ask about things we do not yet know and acquire new knowledge. People that are distinguished and successful in their field are always brave enough to show that they don't know everything. They are self-confident enough, since they know their value and aren't bothered about other people's opinion too much.

If you are a distinguished scientist, you probably dare to admit that you are not good at, for example, cooking or doing laundry. But if you're mediocre, you aren't probably brave enough to admit to others that you cannot cook, because in your eyes it's a confirmation that you fail at anything you do.

One of the best decisions in your life may be if you start living like an adult that doesn't know everything. You don't need to worry about the impression you leave and can acquire knowledge from anywhere you go. You can always ask silly questions, just like children do.

Only those whose cup of wisdom is half-full can learn something new. Your life will take a different turn if you have a childlike attitude no matter where you go and in everything you do. Don't have the know-it-all attitude but be ignorant and willing to learn instead! The real wisdom is not expressed in knowledge but in results. The real wisdom is to admit one's ignorance, to learn everything, and then achieve remarkable results.

I am more than convinced that you can't fulfill your dreams without looking stupid at some point. There is always someone who finds your dream to be irrelevant and absurd. People are so different. I'm always convinced that one cannot be happy without being silly at the same time. You can be yourself and feel free only if you're simple.

Children dare to be simple. They are eager to learn and open to all new things. Grown-ups want to be know-it-alls, but this way, they close doors that lead to new knowledge and experience. One of the best decisions of your life may be becoming as simple as a child!

A STORY ABOUT CHILDISH SIMPLICITY

—

Mark Twain

The real name of the legendary writer Mark Twain was Samuel Langhorne Clemens. The story about how he adopted Mark Twain as his pseudonym is quite peculiar.

Clemens grew up in the city of Hannibal near the Mississippi river, and had dreamt of becoming a captain of a river steamer ever since being child. At the age of 21, he fulfilled his childhood dream, starting to learn how to drive a steamer on the Mississippi. Two years later, he took a full-time position as a licensed steamboat captain.

He loved his job – it was interesting, well paid and with a high social ranking. Driving a steamer involved big responsibility because one had to look out for shoals constantly. In order for the steamer to navigate safely, the river had to be at least 12 feet deep. Since one fathom is approximately 6 feet, the crew members used to shout either "mark one", which meant one fathom, or "mark twain", which was the safe depth of two fathoms or 12 feet. "Twain" is the old-fashioned word for two.

Unfortunately, he was able to be a captain for only two years, as river traffic stopped at the commencement of the Civil War. But because working on the river was so close to Clemens' heart, he adopted the pseudonym Mark Twain for the first time when writing a travel story at the age of 27. From the adult's point of view, a name should be logical and meaningful. But Mark Twain had a childlike frame of mind – he just chose a name that was close to his heart. Since "mark twain" means safe depth, he had definitely associated the term with heartwarming and positive emotions when working on the river.

In any case, the childlike name borrowed from the Mississippi slang became world-famous during his lifetime. And who knows – maybe he would have never written such great books if he hadn't taken the name he loved so much.

"I'VE NEVER LET MY SCHOOLING INTERFERE WITH MY EDUCATION."

–

Samuel Langhorne Clemens

GROWN-UPS WORRY, CHILDREN HAVE FUN

Grown-ups love worrying. Worrying, by its nature, is a relatively negative and non-productive activity. Worrying lets us act out all the possible chaotic scenarios in our heads, each worse than the other, trying to decide which one could become the reality. We focus on uncovering possible problems.

Kids have fun and know little about worrying. They don't know how or want to think what could go wrong. They concentrate on finding solutions with all their senses. Children are innovative and focus on finding new opportunities, not hesitating nor doubting. It is difficult to achieve anything when you worry.

If you have invested all your energy into finding problems, then how can you find creative solutions and enjoy life? If you wish to fulfill your dreams and be happy, you need to concentrate on having fun instead of worrying. Instead of thinking what could go lopsided, start acting with joy and looking for answers; and cross the bridge when you get to it.

Sometimes grown-ups get drunk to experience peace and happiness. Actually, we have the ability to arouse euphoria and a last-

ing sensation of happiness by our childishly positive thinking that intoxication can never offer.

Some grown-ups are incurable worriers. They start worrying the minute they wake up in the morning. What time is it? Maybe I'm late? Should I wear something suitable for the weather? Is my boss in a good mood today? Will I cope with my work assignments? What does my boss think about me lately? Oh my God, maybe I'll have an unpleasant meeting today?

Stress could eat you up before you even get to work. This kind of worrying only adds to your problems and negativity. Worrying involves little positive and very few possible solutions, if any. Unfortunately, the fact is that worriers often discover themselves in the midst of troubling situations, unlike people that don't waste time on worrying. It's unfair, isn't it? Wouldn't it be nice if adults that spend so much energy on worrying could get a happy and satisfying life in return?

The reason why worries never end for the worriers is that the things that people think about most of their time are what they will

get. People attract situations they have concentrated on with their thoughts and deeds. If you are devoted to worrying in an adult manner, in fact new issues will arise.

Be brave and stop worrying. Start having fun and looking for answers, just like a child would. Don't act out all kinds of negative scenarios in your head; focus instead on the results you would like to achieve. If you have fun and act joyfully, worries remain in the background without much effort. Those who have fun will have more reason to be happy. When you encounter difficulties on your path, tackling them joyfully can be playfully easy. If you concentrate on having fun, you feel good, your stress level is low and you can solve problems effectively. By enjoying yourself, I don't suggest that you should act irrationally and without considering the consequences. Enjoying yourself means having a joyful state of mind. You should enjoy life and have fun, not be negative and troubled.

Grown-ups hope that if they make sacrifices and give up having fun for the sake of worrying, life will reward them. Unfortunately, it doesn't work like that. Life only rewards the fun-lovers.

Grown-ups hope to prevent possible issues by worrying, but the problems of a worrier never come to an end. Better start having fun like a child today, and you will playfully overcome the obstacles in your path. By having fun, I mean the state of mind of being positive and enjoying life.

A STORY ABOUT CHILDISH ENJOYMENT

John Lennon

The Beatles are the most commercially successful band in the history of pop music. John Lennon was a founding member of the Beatles and an extremely successful and productive singer and songwriter. In the light of all this, it seems odd that John was a passionate Monopoly player. It can be said that he was addicted to Monopoly. Whenever the Beatles were on a tour, John ensured that he had his game set with him to play Monopoly on planes and in hotels. His favorite lots were Boardwalk and Park Place. As long as he held these two lots, he didn't care about losing the game.

Once, a small group of English and American journalists flew along with the Beatles on their 1964 North-American tour. These included the 35-year-old Art Schreiber, the senior correspondent of Group W, whose expertise was politics and national affairs. Schreiber was puzzling about how to find common ground with a subject so far from his expertise and with the Beatles. In a short conversation, he happened to mention to John that he had played Monopoly some time before. Hearing that, John's laconic cold expression melted into schoolboy enthusiasm. "I've got a board!" he said.

"TIME YOU ENJOY
WASTING, WAS
NOT WASTED."
–
*John Winston
Lennon*

Schreiber recounts that from that moment on, they were constantly playing Monopoly. Sometimes the game lasted until so late that he fell asleep. But John Lennon nudged him and said, "Come on, Art...it's your move." They were occasionally joined by the Beatles' guitarist George Harrison. According to Schreiber, George barely said a word during the game while John was always totally involved and excited.

Lennon found that the music business was similar to a game of Monopoly. In an interview he gave to Hit Parade in 1969, he said, "It's like Monopoly, what with all these bankers – and played around a big table with all these heavies. You know the bit... 'Then I'll give you The Strand or Old Kent Road,' and you say 'No, you give me two houses.' It's just like that."

John Lennon was definitely a childishly playful person. Instead of worrying like an adult would, he played Monopoly. It is obviously impossible to make the best band in the world without having a childlike attitude.

GROWN-UPS LOSE FOCUS, CHILDREN ARE COMMITTED

Children dedicate all their attention to the thing they want. They make no compromises when striving towards their goals. When a child is involved in a game, they don't care if it's time to eat or sleep. They are focused on achieving their goal. Kids cry, stamp their feet, but never lose the sight of their objective. When we grow up, we tend to let ourselves be misguided and do what everybody does, instead of seeing what we really care about. Grown-ups tend to lose focus.

You have one life. Don't waste it, paying attention to everything that everybody else does. Be brave enough to ask yourself childish and important questions. What do you really want? What do you actually like doing? What achievements would you be proud of? Start concentrating on what is important to you and don't spend your energy on random activities. For example, if you don't like partying, you don't have to party every weekend only because others do. But if you like partying more than anything, it would be a sin not to do it. If you like spending time with your family, you should do it and say no to your friends more often, without worrying about disappointing them. If you love spending time with your friends,

try to figure out whether being married with three children is the thing for you. Focus on what's really important for you.

If you wish to achieve outstanding results in some field and if you are made happy by results, you need to be committed on achieving them. You can't rashly waste your energy. You need to make choices and give up activities that don't lead you to your goal. A friend of mine decided to make a career as a manager because he really wanted to be one. At the same time, he didn't change his lifestyle and spent at least two evenings partying each week. As a result, he was often tired at work, and just when he started to get focused and energized on the last days of the business week, another weekend with its parties was there.

Thinking like a child, he would have arrived at the simple conclusion that he should only concentrate on what's important. He should have chosen what he was going to focus on – a career or endless partying. In the end, he chose his career and started partying once or twice a month. Right after fixing his focus, he was able to make better decisions at work and as a result, his career took off.

What had held him back from making that decision earlier was his adult attitude. He gave in to his friends' pressure and forgot to ask himself, like a child would have, what he really wanted. He believed that he had to do exactly what his friends did. Our perception is extremely limited. We can't pay attention to everything. Successful people aren't usually smarter, just more committed. They focus their perception intentionally on something specific.

When a kid eats, he or she eats. When a kid plays, they are totally immersed. When a grown-up eats, they can do a thousand other things at the same time: plan what to do after eating; read the paper; talk on the phone. When grown-ups work, they are talking to their families by phone, making holiday plans or logging in to the social network at the same time.

We should learn from children how to effectively do one thing at a time. Grown-ups believe that they are almighty. We wish to be efficient, but beavering away on several things simultaneously we don't engage in any activity with all our might, and won't therefore achieve outstanding results. If you really want to do something well and be happy, you must learn to enjoy one activity at a time.

How does the dinner taste when you are on the phone at the same time? If you concentrate on eating only, you will absorb the food much better. Your whole body is attuned to eating. This is the key to the whole thing!

Grown-ups do everything simultaneously.
Children are focused on one activity.
If you wish to be happy, you must start
directing your energy to one thing –
the thing you really want to do.

A STORY ABOUT CHILDISH COMMITMENT
—
Neil Armstrong

How did it happen that namely Neil Armstrong became the first man in the world that had the honor to step on the Moon? Why him and nobody else? The answer lies within childlike commitment.

Neil Armstrong was fascinated with flying at an early age. He was playing with model planes at the age of three and went on his first airplane flight when he was five or six. At the age of eight or nine, he was making his own models out of balsa wood. At 15, he had made enough money working at the pharmacy to start taking flying lessons at the Wapakoneta airport in Ohio near his home.

When he reached 16, his career as a kind of test pilot was underway. He flew small planes that had just undergone full motor maintenance by the local mechanic. This allowed Armstrong to log flight hours. After working as a test pilot, Armstrong was a fighter pilot in the Korean War and then he joined the NACA that later became the NASA space agency. By 1969, the 38-year-old Neil Armstrong had flown 200 different types of aircrafts, including various gliders, propeller and jet planes, fighters, helicopters and space rockets.

Armstrong was working as a pilot and a space engineer at the same time. Considering his large number of flight hours and unreserved commitment, he was the logical and best choice for NASA in 1969 to lead the Moon flight. The mission became the natural continuation and culmination of his career, while being the biggest challenge of his life, because when the Apollo 11 crew started landing on the Moon, they suddenly discovered that the computer was unable to perform the landing.

Armstrong employed all the previous experience he had gathered throughout his life, and landed the spaceship Eagle on the surface of the Moon. Stepping on the Moon as the first human was the pinnacle of his career. He was rewarded with this great honor only because he had been committed to his passion, flying, in a childishly self-forgetting manner already since the age of three. While others grew up, went to college and got a desk job, Armstrong continued to focus on what he loved more than anything. Committing to a single thing in a childlike manner led him to changing world history.

"PILOTS TAKE NO SPECIAL JOY IN WALKING. PILOTS LIKE FLYING."

—

Neil Alden Armstrong

GROWN-UPS COMPLAIN,
CHILDREN DREAM

What do you think – at what age does dreaming become a waste of time? At 7? 16? 28? How often do you hear a grown-up say that he was dreaming about something for several hours the other day? The grown-ups I know would say that they could have done something useful with that time. Actually, there is no time spent better than the time spent dreaming. The person we dream of becoming is who we'll become in the future. All changes in our lives actually begin by dreaming.

Grown-ups like to complain, children like to dream. Complaining doesn't take us closer to fulfilling our dreams, while dreaming does. Every moment filled with complaining takes grown-ups further away from fulfilling their dreams. If at all possible, never complain! Complaining is the opposite of dreaming.

Children love dreaming. They like to fantasize about all kinds of things, such as what they'd like to do in the future or what the wife or husband of their dreams is like. Grown-ups, however, have acquired a huge amount of wisdom and experience, and they take a reasonable attitude towards life. But reasonable attitude excludes dreaming, because dreaming is a flight of fantasy. Dreaming is done with the heart.

Dreaming arouses emotions. Dreaming has nothing to do with reason and analysis. Grown-ups that dare to dream move on fast and far. They are people that move towards fulfilling their dreams. It's impossible to really dream about something and not move towards its fulfilment at the same time.

The emotion you get from dreaming is so powerful that it drives us by itself, in the subconscious. While dreaming, our motivation is high and we can tackle the challenges ahead. You can only be happy, if you are driven by dreams. If you don't have dreams, you don't have a higher purpose to move to. It is as if you were standing still, and I'm certain you are not sincerely happy this way.

It's very easy to check if you are really dreaming or not. Real dreaming creates an enormous positive emotion inside of you. You experience euphoria; your body is filled with shivers of excitement. You have certainly felt the sensation as a child, when you were expecting something new and big. Maybe you were waiting for presents on Christmas Eve or went to an amusement park for the first time, or started playing an exciting game with friends. With a childlike attitude, you can definitely dream as an adult as well. If you feel real thrill and excitement, it means you have dreamt well enough. It also means that things will go in motion for you.

In order to have truly positive emotions, you need to dream as realistically as possible. Now, imagine that you are dreaming about your new home. Your task is to think it through in as many details as possible: picture what the home should look like. Play bravely and freely as a child! The more specifically you dream and imagine things and situations, the bigger the emotion you will get. Now that you have figured out in which city district your dream home is located and what the house would look like, start taking real steps towards fulfilling your dream. For example, you can browse sales

ads and find out if a house that meets your vision is for sale. Now call the real estate agent and go see it – regardless of whether you have the money to purchase real estate at the moment. Viewing in itself offers rich emotions. When arriving at the house, you may discover that you don't like it, and from then on, you can imagine what you should change in your dream.

Grown-ups find this game childish and pointless. Is there a point at all to go see a house that you can't afford? Maybe it's difficult to reason, but in reality, it may happen that if you have been going to see your dream houses for a couple of years, you may be able to afford one of them someday. It just happens. It's the power of emotion.

But don't dream too big. Your dream must be big enough to touch your soul and create big emotions. At the same time, it must be affordable so you feel that if you employ all your wit, you will achieve it. If the dream is unrealistic, then deep down you won't believe in fulfilling it. This will, in turn, create a negative emotion instead.

If you are currently living in a two-bedroom flat, it's a bit unrealistic to go viewing castles. But if you are living in a small house, a dream of a bigger and more luxurious house is realistic for you. If you're dreaming of a new car that you can't afford at the moment, call the car salesman and go on a test drive, or rent a similar car for the weekend. It doesn't matter that you're seemingly carelessly wasting money on it. Believe me – it will pay off in the long run. Drive in your dream car and imagine it's yours. If you feel positive anxiety while doing it, you are on the right track – you are really dreaming. Play with your new car, just as a child plays with a toy car at the toy store.

Maybe you have a job-related dream. If this is the case, you should take a small step every day towards fulfilling that dream. For example, initially, you could just dress up in the way you would dress if you worked your dream job. If you keep moving bit by bit every day, your heart will feel that you're on the right path. You will soon have the opportunity to move on in bigger steps. You will notice the right opportunities because your senses are engaged in your dream. If nothing else, try doing childish and senseless small things every day, as long as you are making steps towards the fulfillment of your dream!

It could seem silly at first, but the only way to dream truly and successfully is to do it in a childlike manner. And definitely stop complaining. Complaining is an adult thing, but a totally unproductive thing to do. Every time you put someone down, think – maybe it's out of envy. Is that why you are trying to put down the ones that have dared to dream and achieved something? Those lagging behind complain and make degrading remarks about those that move ahead, such as "he was just lucky", "he was at the right place at the right time", "he knew the right people".

This is actually not true in most cases. Happy people and high achievers are those that just dared to dream in a childlike way, making things start moving. Favorable coincidences and the right people came to them. In reality, they will come to each one of us. The question is rather if we've dreamt of being able to use the right moment or if our senses are tuned to that wavelength. The person you see yourself to be in ten years is who you are in ten years.

In order for our dreams to come true, we must dream, as children do. Bravely and emotionally. Take small steps that take you closer to your dream every day, and soon, you will encounter increasingly better opportunities!

A STORY ABOUT CHILDISH DREAMING
—
Walt Disney

After his movie studio in Kansas City went bankrupt, the 22-year-old Walt Disney took a coach to Los Angeles. He only had 40 dollars and an imitation leather suitcase with a shirt, two pairs of underwear, two pairs of socks, and some drawing supplies to his name. He was ready to make a new start.

After years of hard work, he had created the popular cartoons starring Mickey Mouse and Donald Duck, which helped him to make a name for himself in the movie industry. Despite that, Disney was quite worried, because the short cartoons were not bringing in enough to keep the company afloat. Disney had been on the brink of bankruptcy several times. Now, he had a new big dream that he hoped would save the Walt Disney Company.

In 1934, he announced the audacious plan to produce a full-length animated feature, *Snow White and the Seven Dwarf*, with a budget of about 250,000 dollars. By 1937, the budget of the movie had skyrocketed to 1.5 million dollars, making it the movie with the biggest budget of the year. Disney had to go all out to borrow more money and complete the movie, including mortgaging his house.

The Hollywood media called the project "Disney's Folly", as they didn't believe that the audience would be willing to pay to see a full-length animated feature – and a fairytale at that.

A full-length animated film was something unheard of back then. Even Walt Disney's wife Lillian didn't believe in its success. But when the movie premiered on December 21st 1937, it became an instant hit. *Snow White* earned more ticket sales than any other movie before. On the 50th anniversary of the movie in 1987, New York Times wrote that *Snow White's* ticket earnings totaled 330 million dollars, making it one of the most popular movies of all time.

Walt Disney refused to grow up and kept believing in his dream. The fulfillment of this childlike dream was the start of the triumph of animated movies and the mind-blowing success of the Walt Disney Company. Yes, only childlike people can change the world.

"IF YOU CAN DREAM IT, YOU CAN DO IT."
–
Walter Elias Disney

GROWN-UPS ARE GREEDY, CHILDREN ARE GRATEFUL

The ironic thing is that grown-ups, whose purpose is always to get more, are not usually given very much in life. While people that don't hog stuff for themselves seem to get things easily. This could be called a paradoxical situation.

I'll give you an example about earning money and wealth. The greedy attitude of grown-ups always makes them spend their whole income. But if people could set a part of their earnings aside every month and invest it in the future, even an ordinary person would become wealthy later in life. It's achievable to everyone, but only a few people manage it, as it requires giving up the adult attitude of greediness.

Most of the people that have gathered more money than an average person have done it so with childlike gratitude – saving and investing the profits back into the company, instead of wasting. This is what has helped them get so rich over the long run. Of course, rich people also like to spend, but when a truly rich person buys a Ferrari, it takes up such a small portion of their income that if we compared its percentage of his earnings to the earnings of a regular

person, you couldn't even buy a bicycle for that money. That's why it isn't really wasting in their perspective.

To name some of the most remarkable examples, Warren Buffett, one of the wealthiest people in the world, still lives in a humble house he bought with his wife over 55 years ago, at the beginning of his career, when he was just an ordinary person in the financial sense. Amanico Ortega, the founder and major investor of Ikea, one of the three richest people in the world, doesn't pay much attention to the way he dresses. He usually wears simple and comfortable clothes bearing no labels. It must symbolize a certain childlike attitude and gratitude for what they've got.

At the same time, many of those that aren't so rich wish to surround themselves with increasing amounts of luxury. The desire for luxury, however, seems to push wealth away from them. The reason is that if you have the adult attitude of greed, you are attuned negatively, and push away the things you so desire. But if you have a childlike gratitude towards what life has in store for you, and start

enjoying life with this sincere gratitude, you will start attracting the desirable things more and more.

The over-materialistic attitude makes no one happy. You can dream about beautiful, expensive and nice things, but if you turn them into a life objective, you can't really enjoy them. As a start, you could throw away or give away things at home that you don't use often enough. After getting rid of the redundant things, you will feel light and free. Don't get entangled in material values. Don't be afraid of losing a thing. Things can always be replaced.

Gratitude is by nature a childlike feeling. For example, if things have turned out badly at a certain time, adult greed could grow even bigger than before, because an adult knows that he didn't do well, but someone else did. But children don't need much to feel satisfied, because they don't compare all things and people, and they are happy with what they have at hand. Children could give away every last penny if they had to, but not grown-ups.

In order to be grateful, people need to approach things as simply and childishly as possible, leaving aside rationally analyzing everything, because we can always reach the conclusion that we got too little or something is lacking. This way, we can never feel grateful, and our lives go by in disappointment and bitterness. For example, if a grown-up has a garage, they fill it with stuff and say there's not enough room. Even if they had two garages, it might not make a difference. They can still fill up both garages and feel they lack room. Without thinking that maybe they are keeping too much clutter.

If you want to feel joy and see how your dreams are starting to come true, be grateful about all possible things today. You can start by being grateful for the beautiful day when you wake up in the morning, and that you're alive and well. When you enjoy good service, give a handsome tip. If you're young, feel grateful for your blooming age. If you're old, feel grateful for having seen and experienced a lot. It is worth a lot to be grateful for absolutely everything. Feel a childlike gratitude even for misfortune if you have encountered any recently.

A grateful attitude will get you far and you will do better and better. You just can't fall out of luck if you greet your failures with a childlike gratitude. The secret of all happy and successful people is that they are sincerely grateful for what's happening in their lives. It's one of the most important things that distinguish the happy from the unhappy. It's impossible to be satisfied and happy with one's life, while feeling remorse over things one doesn't have and being greedy as well. Being happy and hogging stuff are mutually exclusive. We won't become happier by having more, but we will by wanting less.

Grown-ups almost always find a reason for coveting more for themselves, feeling they don't have enough.
Kids are grateful even for little things.
Happy people are distinguished from the unhappy mostly by feeling childlike gratitude for anything that life offers them.
They feel grateful even for their failures.

A STORY ABOUT CHILDISH GRATITUDE
—
Leonardo da Vinci

Leonardo da Vinci is especially well-known as an artist who painted a multitude of wonderful paintings, including the Mona Lisa and the Last Supper. Da Vinci was a true genius, because in addition to being a painter, he was also a productive scientist, inventor, writer, sculptor, musician, mathematician, geologist and much more.

Da Vinci's special passion was flying. He invented different flying machines, such as the helicopter, glider, parachute, and the airplane's landing gear. His inventions were mostly theoretical treatises that explained the smallest detail of the invention, but he didn't conduct any experiments himself.

For example, his sketch of a helicopter bears a close likeness to modern helicopters, but it was tested successfully only 400 years after Leonardo da Vinci's time. The mind of the biggest genius of all time is characterized well by his attitude towards animals.

Contrary to the popular understanding of the time, he spread the idea that people shouldn't lord it over animals. In his day and age, people used to believe that animals had been created for the

"HE WHO WISHES TO GROW RICH
IN A DAY WILL BE HANGED
IN A YEAR."
–
Leonardo di ser Piero da Vinci

pleasure of mankind. Attitudes favorable to animals started to spread broadly only in the 18th century.

In today's sense, Leonardo was an animal rights campaigner, but he practiced it hundreds of years before such views became popular. He was way ahead of the time he was living in, judging by his attitude. Giorgio Vasari, the author of da Vinci's biography, talks about the way Leonardo da Vinci went to the market to buy caged birds. Back then, they were sold in abundance at Italian markets, whether for food or as pets.

But Da Vinci bought the birds and instead of using them for some purpose or another, he just let them out of the cages into freedom. If a person that is so incredibly talented and busy finds time to protect animals as a hobby, he definitely possesses a childlike attitude.

Da Vinci felt love and gratitude towards animals, especially birds. He didn't treat them as things, as was common back then. This kind of a grateful attitude helped him to create such wonderful and deeply impressive works that we enjoy to this day.

By the way, hundreds of years later, a pregnant German lady was standing in front of Leonardo da Vinci's painting in an art gallery in Florence, Italy. While the lady was marveling at the painting, she felt her baby move for the first time. The Italian father of the child took it as a cosmic sign and they decided to name the child Leonardo after da Vinci. Maybe it was indeed a sign from the great man of the renaissance era, because the boy grew up to become one of the most talented actors of our time – Leonardo DiCaprio.

GROWN-UPS IGNORE CURIOSITY, CHILDREN FOLLOW THEIR CURIOSITY

Curiosity is encoded in our minds. We crave for new knowledge and experience. People have very different interests, which is why they feel curious about different fields. Children follow their curiosity anywhere it draws them. If they want to know about something, they can't resist their curiosity. Grown-ups tend to ignore their curiosity intentionally. But that is a huge mistake.

If we feel curious about something, it's directly linked to the best attributes of our character, our abilities and potential. We are interested in the fields we are good at. If you follow your curiosity like a child would, it will make you a better person. Your strengths become even stronger. You can only be happy if you follow your curiosity. In other words – if you do what interests you.

Grown-ups have a rational approach to curiosity. They try to bottle it up, because they already have a plan for carving out a career. I'm sure you know somebody who is interested in technology. He would give anything to tinker with cars or repair something. But they may still ignore their interest and do something else with their time, should they find it more useful, for example, by investing

more time in office work. At the same time, a more child-minded adult that is also enthusiastic about technology follows their heart and pursues their hobby. The hobby could become a job in due course. The hobby could also help to apply for the next job or create an unexpected career opportunity at the existing one that is in some way related to the skill you've developed. Even if none of the scenarios above apply, you are definitely a happy person if you are engaged in a hobby you feel attracted to.

What are you curios about? You must never settle for merely being mediocre. You can also not waste or ignore your talent or curiosity. You must follow your curiosity like a child and see where it takes you. Kids don't worry about what they spend their time doing. At a certain age, a person becomes rational in an adult manner and

starts doing things that their mind says is useful. At the same time, we neglect the best part that we are actually really curios about.

A similar thing can happen in a family, for example. The parents may have a child, whose interests are totally different from their own. Sometimes, the parents don't understand their child's needs because they don't sense that someone could want to do a lot of sports or tinker away at a wood shop. Grown-ups have their own vision about the future of the child or spending free time. Some parents wish that their child would take interest in literature and music and start guiding or even forcing the child in that direction. That, however, is not right. The most important thing is to understand what the child likes; this is the interest the parents should encourage and support.

People can be happy and successful only when doing what they're curious about. If a child takes interest in music, the parents should do everything in their power to enable the child to be engaged in music. In the beginning, they might not seem especially talented, but since they're curious, they'll have fun doing it and they will make it in life.

Think about the kind of games you found interesting as a child. Are the games related in some way to what you feel interested in as a grown-up? The things that aroused your curiosity as a child say a lot about what your abilities and interests are as an adult. You have not changed as a person, only developed. Be brave enough to follow your curiosity.

Children follow their curiosity, but as grown-ups, we start making rational choices that won't let us follow our curiosity any longer. This is a great mistake. You can't be happy if you don't follow your curiosity.

A STORY ABOUT FOLLOWING
YOUR CURIOSITY IN A CHILDISH WAY
—
Ray Kroc

At the dawn of his 50th birthday, Ray Kroc, the future founder of McDonald's, was selling Multimixer machines to restaurants. He had been doing this for the past 13 years, but lately, the sales had been dropping. One day, a small restaurant in San Bernardino, California, ordered eight Multimixer machines that could make 40 shakes at the same time. Ray couldn't help himself but to go to California out of his childlike curiosity and see for himself why a small restaurant would require such a big number of machines.

He arrived at a small hamburger restaurant managed by Dick and Mac McDonald. Kroc hadn't seen a restaurant like that before. Unlike other drive-in restaurants of the time, this one was self-catering, there were no seats inside, and the menu only featured hamburgers, fries, drinks and milk shakes. The orders were filled using the conveyor belt method, enabling the customers to get their orders in less than a minute.

Kroc quickly calculated the economic profit derived from efficiency, had there been hundreds of such restaurants all over the country. But when he approached the McDonalds with that idea,

"ARE YOU GREEN
AND GROWING
OR RIPE AND
ROTTING?"
–
Raymond Albert Kroc

the brothers said that they were not interested. Therefore, Kroc offered himself to make it happen for them. The brothers agreed and gave Ray the exclusive rights to sell the McDonald's method. Kroc collected 1.9% on every restaurant's revenue, with 1.5% going to the brothers.

Six years later, Kroc and the McDonald bothers developed differences in terms of future development. Ray was disappointed because despite selling dozens of franchises every year, he could barely cover the expenses of the company with the income and the business model did not produce any profit. Kroc supported a riskier and more aggressive expansion plan, where they wouldn't only sell the restaurant's franchise, but rent the lot under the restaurant as well. Since the McDonald brothers found his new plan too risky, he redeemed their shares, paying both of them a million dollars plus taxes. After redeeming the brothers' shares, Kroc started to apply his strategy, quickly spreading across America. Four years later, the company went on the stock exchange and Kroc became a multimillionaire, his share being worth over 500 million dollars. Today, more than 25,000 restaurants are open all over the world.

A recent study shows that the golden arches of McDonald's are more recognizable than the Christian crucifix. If Ray Kroc had been a wealthy man, who didn't follow his curiosity in a childlike manner, McDonald's would never have been established. He went on a long journey out to California just to find out why someone would order eight milk shake machines. Yet, his childlike curiosity laid the groundwork for McDonald's.

GROWN-UPS WALK,
CHILDREN RUN

When I say that grown-ups walk, it's actually pure flattery. Many people in the developed countries have even given up walking. They drive, fly or commute in other ways, requiring just a minimum effort. Children, on the other hand, are physically very active, much more so than after they have grown up. It's one of the reasons why so many people would enjoy life more as a child than as an adult.

Children constantly run around outside. They need to rush somewhere all the time. Grown-ups lack that zeal, which is why sports is a tedious responsibility for them. Unfortunately, it's impossible to be a healthy and completely happy person without being physically active. The correlations between sports and stress have been confirmed by all sorts of studies. Moving is the basis for healthy eating. Looking at any food pyramid, we see that on the base level, there is moving, and only then the different types of food follow. The most important factor is how much we move. It's even a little more important than what we eat.

Kids move for a reason, they always need to check something out. Even if their goals change or they are running around for no purpose, they move all the same. They run or pedal their bikes as fast as they can, because the rush of play makes them arrive faster. Grown-ups don't feel that rush – we don't need to run to look for a friend that has hidden himself behind a bush. Therefore, we must find another cause for motivating ourselves to be physically active as a child.

Let's start from what kind of a person you are. A competitive person could engage in an activity that allows measuring themselves to others. Turn your training into play. If exercising is a tedious obligation, as it usually is for adults, you will start avoiding it sooner or later. It's important to be enthusiastic about exercising. So, find a goal. It's pointless to spend time on training that doesn't make you excited and enthusiastic.

If you are not a competitive person but enjoy doing things together with others, performing and the elegance of movements, join a dance group. If you like to think and spend time on your own, start taking walks in the forest or riding a bike. If you would like to look fit and muscular, prepare an exercise program and start training at the gym on a regular basis. The opportunities for exercising are countless.

Try various things and steadily look for a way of moving and exercising that suits you. Keep looking until you find it! If you don't want to go to the gym, just walk outside for an hour every day. This is a very healthy activity as well. For example, go shopping or to work on foot. Leave the car a couple of miles away from your

workplace and walk the rest of the way to work. The main thing is that you're physically active, the way you were as a child.

When you move, you will feel the energy growing. Moving fills you with *joie de vivre*, and you'll be ready to face any challenge. Some grown-ups think that physical activities or sports are only suitable for schoolchildren. But they forget that our ancestors had to cover long distances in order to protect themselves from danger and to find food. Men mostly hunted, women gathered. Physical activity is encoded in us. Spending just a few minutes at the shop instead of gathering, after getting there by car, is far too little. Start running again, like you did as a child, and you will become a happy and satisfied person.

As children, we are physically active,
but as grown-ups, we neglect sports or
physical activities. Being physically passive
keeps us from being happy.
Start running again,
like you did as a child!

A STORY ABOUT RUNNING LIKE A CHILD
—
Mahatma Gandhi

Mahatma Gandhi was the leader of the Indian independence move-ment, leading India to long-desired autonomy from the British power. His peaceful demonstrations have served as an example for many human rights activists. But in addition to being the leader of the Indian nation, Gandhi was also a supporter of a healthy lifestyle and he noted that walking is "the prince of all exercise".

At an early age, he was used to covering long distances growing up in India. At the age of 18, he went to study in England to become a lawyer as his parents had wished. For the first three months, he tried to blend into the adult English society. He bought himself suits, practiced the English accent, studied French, took violin lessons and participated in dancing courses.

Yet, after three months of expensive efforts to become an English gentleman, he decided to give it up, calling it a waste of money and time. He quit his courses and spent the rest of the three-year study period as a serious student, leading an extremely simple lifestyle. He took up his childhood habits and covered eight to ten miles in London on a daily basis.

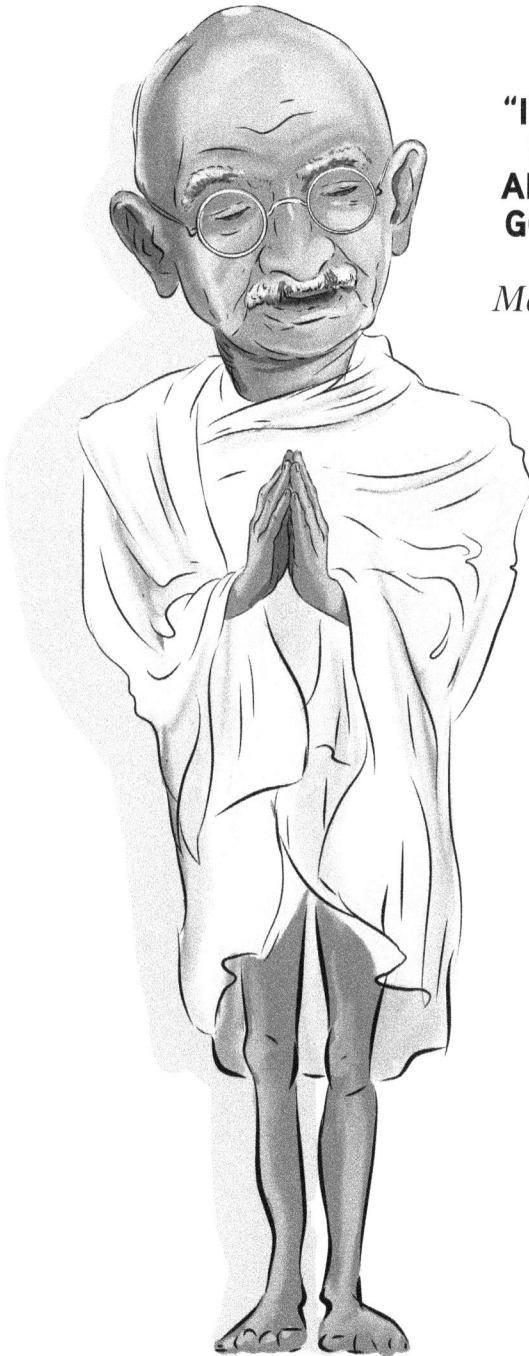

"IT IS HEALTH THAT IS REAL WEALTH AND NOT PIECES OF GOLD AND SILVER."
–
Mohandas Karamchand Gandhi

Years later when he had returned home to India and became popular as a freedom fighter, he was known as a leader that led the same lifestyle as the poorest members of his nation. His aim was to live like his people did.

Gandhi's only garment was a minimalist sheet and he mostly walked barefoot, covering long distances the same way most poor Indians did every day. The Indian people loved their leader for his sincere childlike manner.

When Gandhi was 60 years old, this walking enthusiast decided to organize a 240-mile and a 24-day-long protest march against the English salt tax. With 78 followers, Gandhi launched on a journey from the inland to the coast of the Arabian Sea, where they performed a symbolic salt extraction from the sea, then prohibited by law. On the way to the sea, Gandhi stopped at villages, giving speeches. The villagers joined the march in turn, and eventually thousands of Indians walked to the seashore. As a result of the march, about 60,000 people, including Gandhi himself, were subsequently arrested.

This protest action later helped regain Indian independence. Gandhi was in good health until his tragic death at the hand of an extremist assassin at the age of 78. By then, Gandhi had survived five failed murder attempts. Gandhi's childish enthusiasm in supporting a healthy lifestyle led him, in addition to being healthy himself, to encourage thousands of Indian people to walk, thus expressing their peaceful protest. It may be argued that basically, Indians walked themselves to independence under Gandhi's leadership.

GROWN-UPS HAVE ROUTINE, CHILDREN HAVE ADVENTURES

The word *routine* brings to mind the word *obligation*. The word *adventure* is associated with *opportunity*. It could be said that adults often don't see their lives as adventures, rich in opportunities, but as a series of cumbersome obligations. This way of thinking, however, is limiting and negative. If you perceive your life as highly routine, you won't notice the opportunities that life presents you. But if you see your life as a childish adventure, you will notice them and will be able to be happy.

Adults would be very happy if they could lead their lives by a set routine and fulfill their dreams at the same time. When the safe routine is broken, they may lose their sound footing. Unfortunately, it's a fact of life that you can't get everything good in an instant. If you wish to make your dreams come true, you will need to exchange your adult life based on obligations for a childlike, adventurous life full of opportunities. This way, you will start to expect something new to appear in your life. Nothing new can come to your life if you are clinging to everything old and never deviate from your everyday routine.

Grown-ups see every new day as a tedious pile of obligations: this and that needs to be done, several people need to be met etc. Children, however, see each new day as an adventurous opportunity. The new day promises to be full of discoveries and opportunities. Never say you are bored, because only boring people are bored. Who else but you could make your life exciting? Spicing up our lives is up to us.

In order for you as an adult to be adventurous like a child, you must be brave. You will need to be just a bit fearless – only then will you dare to undertake an adventure that is in store for you every day. The main difference between routine and adventure is that routine involves the familiar and safe, while adventure represents the dangerous and exciting. Familiar and safe things instill a deceitful sense of security. Grown-ups let themselves to be deceived, thinking that the deceitful sense of security provides them with happiness and complacency. In fact, true sense of security and complacency can only be provided by the unfamiliar, uncertainty. The unfamiliar includes new opportunities that take us forward in life. Moving forward will help you experience the true sense of security and happiness.

When you successfully overcome the obstacles in your way, you will feel confident inside. Don't let your adult brain trick you, however – if something seems to be too easy, it usually isn't. Routine is too simple and doesn't offer us any progress or happiness. You will need to become a childlike adventurer that dares to let go of the routine, because only then will endless opportunities find their way to you, and your life will become richer and happier.

You often reach a point in your life where you need to choose between two different paths. One of them is smooth, wide and straight. It will safely and surely take you to the place you already know. The other path is overgrown, narrow and twisty. That path is full of dangers, but will take you to the fulfillment of your dreams. If you dare to accept the challenge and go on a childlike adventure, not turning back at half way, the prize waiting for you at the end will be worth all your efforts.

Grown-ups choose routine over adventure. This, however, rules out new and exciting opportunities that could emerge in their lives. If you wish to fulfill your dreams and be happy, you must be brave enough to let go of your adult routine and go on a childlike adventure.

A STORY ABOUT CHILDLIKE ADVENTURE
—
Albert Einstein

Albert Einstein, the physicist and mathematician, is one of the greatest thinkers in history. The name Einstein is practically a synonym for genius. His discoveries permanently changed our concepts of time, space, substance, energy and gravity, and took the humanity to the next big improvements, such as the introduction of nuclear energy and the exploration of space. The Times magazine declared him to be the person of the century.

But if you think that Einstein was going around all day in a white lab coat with a serious face, you are wrong. Einstein wasn't adult-like and serious, but a scientist with a childlike attitude. For example, he loved sailing. He had been sailing since his youth. Nonetheless, he wasn't by far a masterful sailor, quite the opposite.

Biographers that have studied his life know that Einstein could lose track when sailing, because the legendary scientist often miscalculated. His mast would often keel over; the vessel could run ashore or he might almost collide with other vessels. Several times, Einstein made it on the front covers of newspapers due to his childish sailing adventures because of running aground again or being

E = Energie
m = Masse

$$e = \frac{m \, c^2}{\sqrt{1 - \dfrac{v^2}{c^2}}}$$

"ANYONE WHO HAS
NEVER MADE A
MISTAKE HAS NEVER
TRIED ANYTHING
NEW."
–
Albert Einstein

caught in distress somewhere. Interestingly, he was himself quite indifferent about the dangers related to sailing, which is the more bizarre, considering that he couldn't swim! It's amazing that the famous scientist didn't get drowned.

For example, in 1944, when he was sailing on Lake Saranac in the Adirondack mountains, his boat hit a rock and keeled over. A length of rope got stuck around Einstein's foot and pulled the scientist under the capsized boat for a moment. The sailor-scientist managed to keep calm and get untangled without panicking. That time, a passing motor boat saved Einstein.

Those that knew Einstein more closely knew that he always took a pen and paper with him when he went sailing. This way, he could put down new ideas when he was stuck or when the wind died down. Since Einstein appreciated solitude and privacy, sailing may have been attractive to him because of that feature as well. Maybe it was on board of a sailing boat where he formulated the greatest of his discoveries – the theory of relativity.

Albert Einstein was a truly childlike adventurer. He loved sailing despite not being a good sailor and was therefore often caught in dangerous situations. But danger is inherent in adventure and Einstein was not afraid to face up to it. Einstein was such a remarkable scientist thanks to bravely looking for new adventures, such as sailing, instead of succumbing to routine. That is why he was more creative and open than scientists with an adult's frame of mind. Einstein has said that he created the theory of relativity thanks to his childlike attitude and because he asked the kind of questions that other adults had never asked.

If you're now asking me, what on earth is this theory of relativity all about anyway, I will give you Einstein's childishly simple explanation (too bad physics teachers didn't explain physics to children with such playful examples): "Put your hand on a hot stove for a minute, and it seems like an hour. Sit with a pretty girl for an hour, and it seems like a minute. That's relativity."

GROWN-UPS COMPARE, CHILDREN LOVE

The adult world revolves around sizing up others. They are constantly comparing who gets a higher salary, who has a better wife or husband, who has a more expensive house or car, who has a more interesting job. The grown-ups' world is built on competition. In a way, it can be a driving force, yet, this constant comparing leads to people becoming greedy and negative instead of enjoying the beauty of the game. We will move forward while competing; however, the price we pay is too high. If we acted with creativity and love, though, we would get even further.

We can't stop comparing, and whatever the amount of things we get, we may still discover that there isn't enough. Children, on the other hand, love what they do. Children don't play games only because they want to be better than someone else. They play for fun. They are involved in a game with all their heart. Children are driven by love, whereas grown-ups are driven by comparing. Adults value competition and respect what everybody else seems to do. Individuality as such is not generally highly valued in the grown-ups' world. However, it is namely this childlike individuality that drives

us forward. It is the only thing enabling us to accomplish something outstanding. Paradoxically, those that are driven by competing may not achieve success, while those that concentrate on activities that inspire them, achieve success without it being their ultimate goal.

Children have this unlimited love for their surroundings. They blend in with the world, and the activities and people important to them at that moment. If you can become child-minded like that as an adult, if you can stop competing and love everything around you like a child, you will have reached a higher level – and achieving impossible goals becomes totally possible.

Let's imagine that life is a board game. Grown-ups constantly worry about their position on the board. They are so deep in comparisons that they simply can't see the possibilities that would take them closer to the finish line. Children and child-minded grown-ups, however, are totally involved in the game, so they may not even know exactly where the other players are with respect to themselves. They don't compare but concentrate on the game and use their chances with their whole being. Their creativity is so open that when the

right opportunity arrives, they jump at it immediately, and by doing that take bigger leaps closer to victory. It must be remembered, though, that they are not trying to win at any cost; their aim is to enjoy the beauty of the game. This is how one plays like a child, loving the activity with all their heart.

If you are childlike, you are also creative. You don't waste a moment on comparing yourself to others. Instead, you just enjoy what you are doing and try to do it to your best ability. You are positive and there is anticipation in your soul, you are driven by love.

With a grown-up attitude towards your activities, you will naturally start comparing situations. In the midst of comparing, you switch over to your rational mind to figure out if you are acting in the best possible way. You can start second guessing yourself, become insecure, glum and grumpy. If this negative mood takes you over, simply stop working and go out to have fun. Give your best to reach the childish, loving and caring wavelength. You need to work on your mind frame and attitude. There is nothing worse than the (grown-up) attitude of comparing everything.

Grown-ups waste their productive energy on comparing everything.
Children do things purely out of love, they don't know how to compare or compete.
In order to be happy, you must acquire the mindset of love and creativity.
Then you will enjoy what you do without spending a moment on comparing.

A STORY ABOUT CHILDISH LOVING
—
Wolfgang Amadeus Mozart

The world of classical music owes a lot to Mozart. His work has influenced the works of many later composers, for instance Beethoven. These days, his music continues to captivate music enthusiasts all over the world, and he is considered one of the greatest composers of all time. The Austrian composer's talent was widely known throughout Europe during his lifetime. The following story may be a fabrication, but it sounds authentic, so it may as well have happened in real life.

One day, a young man approached Mozart, wanting to know how to write a symphony. Since the lad was at a very young age, Mozart suggested he compose ballads instead. The young man was surprised at the suggestion and answered, "But you wrote symphonies, when you were only ten years old". "But I didn't need to ask how," countered Mozart.

Whether it is a real story isn't that important. The important thing is that the world is full of people with an adult attitude that compare themselves to the geniuses of various walks of life. The cocky answer Mozart gave could have been caused by him loving

"NEITHER A LOFTY DEGREE OF INTELLIGENCE NOR IMAGINATION NOR BOTH TOGETHER GO TO THE MAKING OF GENIUS. LOVE, LOVE, LOVE, THAT IS THE SOUL OF GENIUS."

–

Johannes Chrysostomus Wolfgangus Theophilus Mozart

composing from the bottom of his heart. He worked enthusiastically and relentlessly on every single note until he achieved complete harmony. This kind of focus is only possible when loving your job without reservation like a child, and it cannot be learnt by mimicking others.

We may suppose that the youth wanted to earn the kind of recognition Mozart received. He desired to achieve the same kind of results, while not probably loving writing music to the same extent as Mozart did. Otherwise, as Mozart replied, he shouldn't have had to ask how to write symphonies.

Those that love their work and things they create like a child concentrate on their activity with all their might, without wasting time on comparing themselves to others, like an adult does. If that young man had loved his work with all his heart, he wouldn't have even thought of comparing his progress to some other creator, for his attention would have been concentrated on loving his own work. Only by loving like a child is it possible to put your heart in what you create and achieve outstanding results.

GROWN-UPS' EYES ARE DIM, CHILDREN'S EYES ARE BRIGHT

Go through your albums and find a few photos of yourself. The best photos to illustrate my point are those that were taken when you were not posing but you caught unexpectedly, in your natural state. Today, you have those photos in your pocket – just take out your mobile phone and open the photo gallery. Take a look at your photos and observe the eyes. Are your eyes dim or bright?

The eyes of adult-minded people are dim, while the eyes of childlike people are bright. Eyes are the mirror of one's soul. If your eyes shine, your soul also shines. If your eyes are dim, your soul is also dim. If you discover that your eyes are dim when looking at your photos, then think about the reason why. When have you felt that your soul and eyes are shining brightly?

In the future, don't place yourself in situations that make your eyes go dim. Children's eyes are almost always bright. Yet, the question is rather at what age one's eyes stop shining. In the case of some childlike people, their eyes won't stop shining even at a very old age. In others, they lose the shine in their eyes already at school age. The simplest way of knowing childlike and happy

people is to observe their eyes. If a person hides their eyes or if their eyes nervously avoid other people's glaze, or are just dim, they are unhappy.

Don't let yourself be distracted by a smiling face or seemingly joyful chatter. Concentrate on the eyes and it will be clear if the person is happy inside. Look at the eyes of outstanding people. Follow those that are childlike and have achieved remarkable results. Usually, the eyes of that kind of people are extremely playful and bright. You might even say that the meaning of life is living with bright eyes. The extra bonus of that shine is the fact that shining eyes make a person at any age more beautiful. Live so that you feel that your eyes are shining!

The eyes of adult-like people are dim, those of childlike people, however, are bright. Don't let the shine of your eyes go dim. Live a childlike life, one that lets you feel the shine in your eyes!

A STORY ABOUT CHILDISHLY SHINING EYES

—

Sophia Loren

The story of Sophia Loren, the actress of the golden era of Hollywood, who was considered one of the most beautiful women in the world, resembles the fairytale of the Ugly Duckling. She was born in 1934 in Rome and was raised by her mother in Pozzuoli, a small town in Italy. Sophia's childhood passed in poverty. She and her mother shared a single bedroom with six other relatives. When the already poor town was destroyed in the Second World War, her family had to live in destitution. The situation could get so bad that they were forced to draw water from the car radiator that their mother then fed to her daughters in turns. Loren had a thin and strange figure; her classmates called her "little stick".

But everything changed for Loren at the age of 14, when she blossomed overnight and turned from thin as a rake into a beautiful and curvy woman. That year, Loren participated in the Miss Italy 1950 beauty competition, and a year later, her mother took her to Rome, so that her daughter could start earning a living as an actress.

At the age of 23, Loren's career as an actress was underway in Hollywood. When she played in the movie, *The Pride and the*

"BEAUTY IS
HOW YOU FEEL
INSIDE, AND IT
REFLECTS IN
YOUR EYES. IT IS
NOT SOMETHING
PHYSICAL."
–
*Sofia Villani
Scicolone Ponti*

Passion, with Cary Grant and Frank Sinatra, she got entangled in a love triangle when Cary Grant, the most desirable man of the time, and Carlo Ponti, the Italian movie producer, asked her to marry them at the same time. Cary Grant and Sophia Loren could have been a Hollywood dream couple. But even though Grant deeply impressed Loren, she eventually chose the movie producer Carlo Ponti – a man the media joked was twice Loren's age and half her length. Ponti was a middle-aged man, 22 years older than Loren, and already married on top of everything.

For outsiders, the union didn't seem to be the right nor very romantic in any sense. But Loren didn't care about other people's opinions when getting married. Sophia Loren and Carlo Ponti were happily married for 50 years, until he passed away in 2007. Their marriage is still one of the most heart-warming success stories among the relationships of the Hollywood celebrities. Loren herself has said that the secret of their relationship was keeping a low profile despite of being famous. "Show business is what we do, not what we are," she has said.

Sophia Loren followed her heart in a childlike manner when choosing a husband. If she had followed her mind, she could have picked Cary Grant. This union would have definitely promoted her career as an actress. She didn't choose this "appropriate" man, picking instead a man that brought out the best woman in her. We should make these kinds of childlike choices in our lives, so that our eyes could shine.

Cary Grant, however, married five times in his life. Quite the contrary to his movie characters that were always smooth with ladies, he probably never found true happiness in real life.

GROWN-UPS TRUST REASON, CHILDREN ARE INTUITIVE

Grown-ups are constantly trying to sort their memory images to compare the present moment to their earlier experience and make the best decisions in the present. This is a very adult thing to do, but totally useless! Experiences are stored inside us anyway, and going through our memories won't enable us to use them effectively. We can only use our previous experience to the fullest when we trust our intuition, just like children do.

Since children don't have much experience yet, they need to trust their intuition. Intuition is quicker and often more accurate than reason. Look at some great discoveries and important decisions, for example – they have been instantaneous flashes rather than the result of long analysis. All important groundbreaking and right decisions are actually born in a childlike, intuitive manner. We trusted ourselves when we made a decision. The more experience and knowledge we have, the more accurate our intuition becomes. That explains why some people are more successful at relying on their intuition than others – they just have more experience in a specific field. Intuition also becomes

more accurate when we have developed a habit of trusting our inner voice.

Scientific research also proves that quick, childlike decisions, made based on the gut feeling, can often be more to the point than those made after long analysis. Scientists explain the precision of intuition with the fact that when we trust our instincts, we turn to knowledge that we didn't know we possessed. That knowledge is stored in the subconscious, but we can't always restore it by logical reasoning. Intuition doesn't work like the mind, but only gives us an answer, never giving any explanations.

The simplest way of listening to our inner voice is to simply follow the emotion that springs up in us. Children act just like that – they make a decision according to their emotions. When we have a warm and positive emotion in connection with a person, a decision or something else, we are on the right track. But if something makes us restless, nervous or creates a negative emotion, we should trust that feeling, even if the facts may show that everything's ok. The rational mind is much easier to distract with facts than our intuition. Our gut feeling sees beyond facts and senses the whole that the mind could never do without intuition. When intuition gives us an answer, our rational mind will never be able to explain it.

When swerving towards a certain decision, we can't present any logical arguments in its defense. But the mind can never keep up with intuition. That is why it's inexplicable to the mind, why we are able to choose intuitively an ideal wife or husband or pick a specialty, where we have a good outlook to shine, or how we can make the only correct decisions in critical situations. The more you trust your intuition in a childlike manner, the more intuition will help you as well.

All outstanding people have acted intuitively. Without trusting your intuition, you are like a three-wheeled car. A three-wheeler can lose control in the next big curve, however, when life makes a small turn to the left or right. Grown-ups have an irresistible urge to get their life under their control. They wish to systematize and categorize everything in a sensible manner and then arrive at the right decision by the scientific method. Figuratively speaking, we place all information in jars, label and store them, and then take out the correct jar at the right moment. But this method is very slow and misleading.

Like the saying goes, "We make plans, God laughs". It refers to the fact that even the seemingly smart, rational and in every sense highly intellectual people cannot always be happy nor achieve remarkable success in their chosen activity. Reason has become their obstacle.

Reason in itself is quite valuable indeed – the more wisdom, the better. But grown-ups use reason in a wrong way. You don't have to become the smartest; you just have to able to use reason in the right way. Don't turn your mind into a supreme God or Big Guide, but trust your inner childlike intuition and use it when making decisions. Don't worry about not being a real genius, or if you weren't standing out for extraordinary results at school. If you are childlike and dare to trust your intuition, you are actually smarter than the people that trust reason in everything. Your will have a far happier and more meaningful life.

The more you trust your intuition in a childlike way without asking questions, the happier and more successful life you will have.

A STORY ABOUT CHILDLIKE INTUITION
—
Margaret Thatcher

The opinion polls of the beginning of 1982 showed that Margaret Thatcher was the most unpopular Prime Minister of the United Kingdom of all times. Very few believed that she could ever lead her party to victory again. A year later, however, Thatcher won the election, beating her competition by a huge margin. The events of 1982 were what helped Margaret Thatcher become one the most remarkable and influential politicians of the 20th century.

That single year was an absolute turning point in Thatcher's career. But what exactly happened back then?

On 2 April 1982, the Argentinean forces occupied the British Falkland Islands in the Southern Atlantic. The invasion came out of the blue for the government of the United Kingdom. Prime Minister received intelligence on the invasion only two days before the attack. Since the island was still inhabited by residents that preferred the status of an overseas territory of the UK, Thatcher had to decide what to do about the Argentinian invasion.

On the night before 31 March, catastrophe was evident. Thatcher faced humiliation and possible resignation from the office. She

"I USUALLY MAKE UP MY MIND ABOUT A MAN IN TEN SECONDS, AND I VERY RARELY CHANGE IT."
–
Margaret Hilda Thatcher

was personally responsible for the United Kingdom not being able to protect her islands against the intrusion. Using her intuition, Thatcher made the radical decision that night that the United Kingdom would enter into a full-scale war to protect the Falkland Islands. Her decision met strong opposition and critical statements from both her opponents, members of government and even her own party. For example, one of the Prime Minister's counsellors held the position that "we are making a big mistake", others suggested "blowing up a few ships and nothing more". Sir John Hoskyns, Thatcher's political advisor said that the government was making a fool out of itself and the war decision would lead to the collapse of the Thatcher regime.

The general opinion was against Thatcher's decision and she was advised to find another solution. But using her childlike intuition, Thatcher felt that it was necessary to act decisively and saw the conflict differently from most members of her government and party.

The war brought out Thatcher's best features – she found creative solutions, made fast intuitive decisions and won the Falkland war that lasted for 74 days. Falkland changed everything for Thatcher. It became a turning point in her career – the nation backed her now, because she had been right. She could have reached that decision – correct in hindsight – only by her childlike intuition. All the facts, advisors and analyses became totally useless. She followed her emotions and based on her gut feeling, made a decision that was the right one for the nation of Great Britain. The childlike bravery to follow her intuition lifted Thatcher to a higher level compared to a regular head of state. A level that can be achieved only by childlike people.

GROWN-UPS ACCEPT THE SITUATION, CHILDREN THROW A TANTRUM

I cannot tell at what age we start accepting situations and making compromises. At one point, we just give up our dreams and accept the reality. Some childlike grown-ups never accept the current situation. They throw tantrums like children and make their wishes come true with those tantrums.

In order to be happy, you need to start throwing tantrums. If you let life walk over you and won't make a fuss about it, you can never be happy or achieve anything significant. Grown-ups like being well-mannered and not sulk. That behavior is based on wisdom, being considerate of others, politeness and other good qualities. Unfortunately, it's impossible to be truly happy when you dance to the tune of the general public. Therefore, you need to throw tantrums like a child that is not happy if he or she won't get their way. But since you are an adult, instead of trampling and screaming, you act – in the right direction, productively.

As a grown-up, you can sulk in a more civilized way. I would call it intelligent or productive sulking. You are obstructive, because you don't accept a certain situation. And if you don't accept it, it means

you will do something to change it. By changing, you in turn live to the fullest. Now, you will experience success and you have a reason to be pleased with yourself.

Many adults are as meek as sheep, accepting whatever is offered to them without protest. It might be that this behavior is linked to a kind of feeling of martyrdom. But don't be a victim! Make your own luck, start sulking and do things differently. Do them in a way that is necessary to you and how you see fit.

Throwing tantrums reveals your true wishes in a way, and shows what you really want. Every time you suppress your sulking, you give up a tiny piece of your life. There is still obstruction inside of you, despite the fact you don't show it. You just accept the situation and become more miserable.

I can't say why so many adults just look at the situation and say, "That's life". Children would say, "Life is what you make it." Grown-ups would make a list of logical and intelligent arguments that would justify their miserable situation. In fact, it's just a wish to be humble and accept the situation. Grown-ups lack courage to sulk and change the status quo.

Next time you plan to give up, saying that there's nothing for it, it is what it is, just start sulking instead. Tell yourself and others that you are unhappy and about to make some changes. Do it even if you don't exactly know at that exact moment how you could turn the situation in your favor. In any case, you should throw tantrums like a child, in order to let your true nature show. You need to start satisfying your needs instead of suppressing them. Be obstructive, change the situation, and you will soon feel a taste for life and the transforming force of childish tantrums! If you are childlike, you won't stop before you will have found what you are looking for!

Instead of throwing tantrums, grown-ups turn their backs and accept the situation. Every time you refuse sulking, you are as if giving away a tiny piece of the life you could have had, if you had rebelled against life and been obstructive like a child.

A STORY ABOUT CHILDISH SULKING
—
Michelangelo

Even after making the sculptures "David" and "Pieta", which brought him much fame and recognition, Michelangelo still had to tussle over commission fees with customers like Doni. Doni was a Florentine merchant. He commissioned the oil painting, *Tondo Doni*, but didn't want to pay a fair price for it. This enraged Michelangelo.

Giorgio Vasari, a biographer of Michelangelo, writes that when the sculptor had finished painting the panel (it was a wood panel, not a canvas), he nicely wrapped the painting and asked his servant to deliver it to Doni. "How beautiful!" exclaimed Doni, when he opened the package. "How much does the master want for it?" "Seventy ducats," the servant replied. Silence. Doni was shocked by the price. He loved decorating his house with nice paintings, but he could have got some truly useful things for seventy ducats. The sum crossed the line. He had bought a copy of an Ancient Roman faun for eighty ducats – and that was antique. This young artist, who was not even a painter but a sculptor, had some nerve to ask that much for a simple painting.

"Here's forty," Doni said to the servant. "That's plenty. Tell the master that the painting is very beautiful." Half an hour passed, while Doni was waiting for news. "That Michelangelo knows that he asked too much," he thought. "When he sees forty ducats, he will be happy enough".

A knock on the door. Michelangelo's servant appeared with a message: "My master said that you have to return the painting or pay a hundred ducats." "Is your master nuts? He only asked seventy before." "Now he wants a hundred. You may also return the painting to him, Sir." Doni gave it some thought. He looked at the painting on the chair next to the window. It depicted the Holy Family in a very original way. He had planned to surprise his guests and hang the painting over the dining table.

"Alright," he said. "Tell your master that he is a greedy man and it's his fortune that the rest of us value other things besides money. Here's another thirty ducats. Now, he gets his seventy." For the next fifteen minutes, Doni studied the painting in more detail. "That little boy that is looking up towards the sky behind Saint Joseph's back must be Saint John," he thought. "And those naked boys in the background – who are these? Whatever. It's a beautiful painting with a few mysteries – it's exactly what I like: originality, mystery. The damned thing is probably worth two or three hundred ducats, so congratulate yourself, mister Doni." A knock on the door. Michelangelo's servant was again at the door.

"The Master said that you have to return the painting or pay the remaining seventy ducats. His price is one hundred and forty ducats." Doni turned red with anger. "It's twice as much as the original price. Does he think I'm crazy?" Doni addressed the guests that had arrived in the meantime and were sitting in the fancy atrium of his house, amused by watching the funny bargaining. "Those artists are the most shameless people on earth. I think I will simply return his ugly painting. Florence is full of paintings of the Holy Family – does he think he's some sort of a special genius?

"FAITH IN ONESELF IS THE BEST AND SAFEST COURSE."
–
Michelangelo di Lodovico Buonarroti Simoni

He should be happy if someone pays him ten ducats and no more. I've had enough."

Doni asked his servants to wrap the painting up once more. The guests sitting in the atrium included Doni's neighbor, who was also a collector of rare and beautiful things. He was more excited about the painting than Doni himself. While the servants were wrapping up the painting in order to return it to the artist, Doni suddenly realized that Michelangelo could by all means sell it to someone else now. And his neighbor, the dirty wheeler-dealer, could purchase it for himself – would he really dare?

Doni became envious and changed his mind about returning the painting. "Come into my study," he quietly told the messenger and went out of the hearing range of his guests. "Tell your master that I have crossed my limit. Here's another forty ducats. It's much more than the artist could even dream his painting is worth, because it's forty ducats more than he originally asked." The servant didn't raise his hand to accept the money.

"Don't you know," he said. "My master is furious at you. When I told him the news that you had given forty instead of seventy, it seemed as if he was possessed with evil spirits. He said that when you ordered the painting, you promised to pay the sum he asked for and he gave you a fair price. But you tried to deceive him. Now, as a punishment, he has doubled the price. I'm sure that he won't accept a penny less." Hearing that, Doni finally paid the remaining seventy ducats.

Michelangelo threw a childish tantrum to get what he wanted, because he knew that he was right. His childish sulking led him to painting the ceiling of the dignified Sistine Chapel that became his masterpiece. Michelangelo didn't accept injustice, but started trampling and fussing. This childish fussing made him one of the greatest artists the world has ever witnessed.

GROWN-UPS SEEM TO BE OPEN, CHILDREN ARE TRULY OPEN

Grown-ups love making it look as if they were open persons. They talk to each other in a friendly way; some details about their lives are slipped in the conversation, creating a trusting atmosphere. In reality, they don't really open themselves, but merely chat. I will prove it to you with a simple question. How well do you really know your friends?

Our beloved ones can often surprise us with things we had no idea about. Often, the parents don't really know their own children, if they have never had heart-to-heart conversations with them. The more developed the society, the more there is chatter and less talk about what really touches the soul. Grown-ups are afraid of opening themselves, because their frankness can be abused later on. Children can't think like that. They say straight and honestly, what they have on their minds. But adults make their lives difficult, saying the pre-conceived things that could benefit them in the future.

When grown-ups fall out, it may last for long and become very tiring, because both parties hold back, hiding their true thoughts and emotions. Grown-ups actually make things worse by keeping

their opinion to themselves, because the fight will go on under the surface. The emotions kept under the lid in an adult way will surface later, for example as uncontrolled bursts of anger. Children can't fight like that. When children fall out, they speak their minds there and then, and on the next day, they can forget about the dispute having cleared the air, and make up.

In most cases, the grown-ups' actions have specific motives. They often leave aside the important fact that one should just live in the moment, enjoy the conversation and open oneself. The chess game-like conversation, where our purpose is to never slip and only say the right things, indeed prevents any risk – we will probably not step on anyone's toes. This kind of a soulless conversation, however, doesn't offer us anything, which is why we can certainly not be happy either.

By speaking only what others like to hear and by not opening yourself, you will always remain an average and unhappy person whose true nature remains secret to others. Leaving a specific impression of ourselves and only mimicking being an open person

means we will never experience true friendship or love. We won't have true friends, only a large circle of acquaintances for empty chatter. Once you start opening yourself in a childish and sincere way, you take a certain risk. Now that you take your mask off and start saying what you really think, not everybody will like you anymore. First impressions take the biggest hit because those that don't know you yet won't understand that you are speaking from your heart. They may confuse openness for arrogance – because most grown-ups don't speak their minds.

But the risk is worth it, because when you open yourself in a childish way, you will start winning over real friends that appreciate you for real. You will be seen as charismatic. If you think about any outstanding person that many people appreciate, he or she is most likely a sincerely open person. When performing their duties, they may not always be open, because the unwritten etiquette of their profession doesn't foresee it. But among friends and family, they are surely very open compared to regular people.

They would never have reached their current position if they hadn't found allies that support them. But true allies can only be found if people open themselves for real. Speaking about their ambitions, values and plans in a childish and honest way, they found the right companions to go on with. If they had been satisfied with small talk, they would never have become the personalities they are today. Openness, of course, also has limits, and one has to be careful about when, where and to whom one opens up, because candor can be abused. But we need to be totally open with at least someone. We need to have an inner circle. We can't be closed to the whole world, because then we'll have no one to rely on.

For example, think about presidents and prime ministers – they are people that have led the history's greatest nations. Some may think that they are the last people to rush to show their true nature to others. When watching the leader of a world superpower speaking on television, it may seem that their speeches are carefully thought through and prepared by many people.

How did they achieve their position in the first place? Without exception, all great statesmen have long before dreamt about rising to power and shared their vision with their companions. Dreaming in this sincere and childish way, and involving others in their dreams, they have been truly open – they have shared the innermost thoughts of their soul with others. There were plenty of those as well, of course, who laughed at their ideas.

There are many mockers and people with an arrogant attitude who think of personalities with big dreams as simple-minded fools. But that is the price of the risk you take. You can, of course, be silent like an adult and secretive with your companions, but then you will never fulfill your dreams. All great people can attest that fate has eventually guided them to the right people who didn't ridicule their dreams and believed in them.

If you wish to live happily and make your dreams come true, you will have to risk and open yourself truly and childishly. By only faking to be open in an adult way, we will not make true friends and allies, only a large number of acquaintances for small talk.

A STORY ABOUT CHILDISH OPENNESS
—
Rafael Nadal

Rafael Nadal is considered to be one of the best tennis players of all time. If you switch on any sports channel on the TV, you can see Nadal, a fearless and superhuman tennis warrior, who is a ruthless opponent to his rivals.

Francis Roig, an ex-professional tennis player, has given a very apt description of Nadal: "The simple action of wrapping on his bandanna is so frighteningly intense; his eyes, far away, seem to see nothing that's around him. Then, suddenly, he'll breathe deep and kick into life, pumping his legs up and down and then, as if oblivious to the fact that his rival is just a few paces away across the room, he'll let out a cry of "Vamos! Vamos!" ["Let's go! Let's go!"]. There's something animal about it. The other player may be thinking his own thoughts but he won't be able to help casting him a wary sideways glance – I've seen it again and again – and he'll be thinking, "Oh, my God! This is Nadal, who fights for every point as if it were his last. Today I'm going to have to be at the very top of my game, I'm going to have to have the day of my life. And not to win, just to have a chance.""

"I ALWAYS WANTED TO BE HONEST WITH MYSELF AND TO THOSE WHO HAVE HAD FAITH IN ME."

–

Rafael Nadal Parera

Now, try to imagine that in addition to a brave tennis warrior, there is also a totally different Nadal. Not the best tennis player in the world – Rafael Nadal – but just Rafa, whose true nature is known to all his close ones and the loyal fans. As he says about himself, "I am not the most courageous guy in the world outside of the court."

After losing to Roger Federer in the Wimbledon final in 2007, Rafa went to the locker room and cried his heart out for half an hour straight. Rafa is afraid of dogs and other animals. He doesn't like darkness, which is why he prefers to leave a lamp or the TV on when he is asleep at night. He also doesn't feel comfortable during thunder storms. Rafael drives his car extremely carefully, and for a good reason, because as his sister says, he is a "terrible driver".

Rafa refuses to swim if his feet can't touch the bottom, and his biggest fear is that something could happen to his close ones. Sometimes, he sends text messages or calls his sister ten times a day and gets twitchy when he gets the slightest suspicion that he could have fallen ill. With an adult attitude, Nadal would hide his weaknesses and try to seem like a perfect person. He could also ask his close ones to help and conceal his shortcomings.

But Nadal's attitude is totally open in a childish way. He is always honest to himself and others, and never conceals his weaknesses. For example, if a regular grown man that is afraid of dogs would encounter one, he would probably try to quietly find an excuse to walk away. But if Nadal encounters a dog, he is likely to tell you that he is afraid of your dog. Nobody would ever have found out that he cried in the locker room of Wimbledon if he had hidden it himself.

If you ask him something, you will receive a totally honest answer. It's proven by countless press conferences, where he has caused a sensation with his childish openness. When Nadal is victorious in an important match, he falls on the court without noticing it himself and cries tears of joy. That's because he doesn't try to conceal his nature and emotions. He lets the emotions loose without worrying about the impression it leaves to others.

By only pretending to be open in an adult way, he would never have made it because he wouldn't have had the total understanding and support of his loved ones. But his family's support is the most important thing to Nadal according to himself. Only by facing and sharing his fears, shortcomings and dreams with his family, he has managed to reach the point in tennis where he is today – the absolute top of the world of tennis.

GROWN-UPS DON'T BELIEVE, CHILDREN BELIEVE

Children are much more religious than grown-ups are. Faith requires us to believe us in something without our minds doubting it. We just believe. It is much easier for children, because they don't think rationally like grown-ups do. Grown-ups are rather distrustful, logical and reasonable. But any type of logics and doubting prevents us from believing from the bottom of our hearts.

For example, let's imagine that we dream about doing something great and unique. If we approach the idea in a childish way, it's easy to believe in the dream with everything we have. As adults, however, we start dissecting the dream in our minds and look for logical links. It will turn out that our dream has some weaknesses. From that moment on, we start doubting and our mind starts telling us that nobody has ever done anything like that before, so it's unlikely that I could be the first one to do it, that I'm not talented enough etc.

We can always find logical excuses, but in fact, every person that has achieved something great and incredible in their life is just like everybody else. Take a close look at a top player in any field and you will see that it's an ordinary person in every sense. They don't have special talents or major advantages, but they do have a significant difference compared to regular people. They have much greater belief in themselves and their goals. That belief is childish, naïve, and uncompromising. Keep that thought in mind. Next time you start doubting yourself, that fact will help you to find your footing and move on.

One can only truly believe in a childish way. One needs to put a stop to the reasonable complex analyses and trust only the gut feeling. Gut feeling tells us without a doubt whether our plan can be realized or not – assuming that we have enough childish courage

and faith. Trust your gut, and don't listen to your doubting mind. The mind always tries to find logical reasons why one or another dream cannot come true.

Let me give you an example. Imagine that you and your small child are driving in the large parking lot of a super market with no free spots. The weather is extremely bad; it's raining cats and dogs. Nobody wants to walk a long way or park their cars far from the door. Circling around, you drive past the parking spaces near the door. They're all taken. Suddenly, your child tells you that you should drive near the entrance again because there are probably some free spots there by now. You may argue with the kid, but you still drive to look. There are no free spots. After some circling, your

child tells you again that there is definitely a free space near the door now. The kid truly believes this. But the adult reasons that it must be illogical that a space has been freed in this short period. To humor the child, after arguing about it for a short while, you drive back to the entrance looking for a free spot. And lo and behold, on the third attempt, you find a parking space right next to the entrance!

It's a typical and figurative example of shifting the reality when you sincerely believe in something. If you're a childlike person, there is always a free parking space for you near the door when it's raining. If you think rationally like an adult, you restrain your faith and refuse to accomplish seemingly impossible things that are in fact feasible.

Children believe sincerely and without
reservation, because they are not restrained
by their rational and logical attitude.
There is no logic in real faith. It is impossible
to truly believe thinking like an adult.
If you wish to accomplish
something remarkable,
you will need to believe as children do,
sincerely and without any doubts,
trusting your gut feeling.

A STORY ABOUT CHILDISH BELIEF

—

Jesus Christ

A man once went to the barber to have his hair cut and beard trimmed. When the barber started working, they started talking. They talked about various things and on different subjects. When they finally reached the topic of God, the barber, being an adult, said, "I don't believe God exists."

"Why do you say that?" asked the customer.

"Well, you just need to go out in the street to realize that God doesn't exist. Tell me, if God existed, would there be so many sick people? Would there be abandoned kids? If God existed, there wouldn't be pain or suffering. I can't imagine a loving God that would allow all these things to happen."

The customer gave it some thought but didn't answer, as he didn't want to start an argument.

The barber finished his work and the customer left the barbershop. When leaving the shop, he saw a man with long greasy hair and untrimmed beard. He looked dirty and unkempt.

The customer returned to the barbershop and told the barber, "You know what? There are no barbers."

"SO I SAY TO YOU, ASK AND IT WILL BE GIVEN TO YOU; SEARCH, AND YOU WILL FIND; KNOCK, AND THE DOOR WILL BE OPENED FOR YOU."

–

Jesus of Nazareth

"How come?" asked the surprised barber. "I'm here and I'm a barber. And I just served you!"

"No!" exclaimed the customer. "There are no barbers, because if they existed, there wouldn't be people with dirty long hair and untrimmed beards outside, just like the man out there."

"Well, but barbers DO exist!" said the barber. "The truth of the matter is that all people just don't come to me."

"Exactly!" the customer said. "That's it! It's the same thing with God. He DOES exist. It's just that people don't go to Him or look for Him. That's why there is so much pain and suffering in the world."

GROWN-UPS STAGNATE, CHILDREN SEEK DEVELOPMENT

Children are characterized by constant development. They want to learn and move forward. But grown-ups think that they are already big and don't need to develop any further. Actually, the truth is that development is equal to happiness. One cannot be happy without personal development. People need challenges and obstacles in order to feel alive and active. The urge to strive towards something is encoded in a human. As soon as someone's life loses purpose, they become dull and apathetic. Lack of opportunities of development is one of the main reasons for being unhappy.

If you wish to be happy, give up being comfortable in a grown-up manner. Become childish and seek opportunities for developing. Place yourself willingly in situations that make you test your boundaries and become better than before. Grown-ups are often miserable due to the lack of a goal to achieve. Grown-ups give up on their goals because they are afraid of criticism in case they should fail. The fear of failing is so great that it makes people choose mediocre solutions. Holding one's ground and achieving something special requires a large amount of childish naivety and carefree attitude towards life.

In Hollywood movies, it often happens that once the main characters have overcome different challenges during the movie and solved difficult situations, they finally reach a happy ending. It seems as if the protagonists could now enjoy eternal life of ease and happiness. But there are no such moments in real life. We can never enjoy a happy ending where we have to do nothing ourselves.

Life is endless aspiration and development towards a goal. Only by constant movement towards your goals can you be complacent and happy. Grown-ups tend to forget this fact, and so they only live in their daily routine, closed and unchanging. It is as if they were living in a cocoon, without daring to try something new. This behavioral pattern is followed to prevent any kind of failure. In reality, fear of failure is much greater than the failure

itself. It can be compared to fear of the dentist. The fear of pain while teeth are being repaired is much bigger than the actual pain itself.

Children, however, are not afraid of failure. They dare to develop and get into new, unfamiliar circumstances. Having a childish attitude towards life, you as an adult can also taste life and be happy. Try to find ways of developing your skills and test your abilities. All happy people are constantly looking for opportunities of getting new exciting experiences.

Children begin each day with anticipation. There are new games and interesting situations and experiences ahead. Children feel attracted to everything new and interesting. Grown-ups don't often give in to this internal drive that is pushing their development forward. They analyze all their chances with a sober and rational mind and calculate whether the planned activity would be profitable or not. If that reasoning reveals that the attempt may fail, it seems much more reasonable not to take any chances at all. But kids don't analyze everything. They intuitively seek opportunities of development. They are looking for exciting challenges.

If you wish to live a happy life, you must place yourself in new exciting situations just as children do. Embrace excitement and new games. Sign up for an interesting training club, ask your boss for an opportunity to prove yourself in a new project, go hiking or learn a new skill. Don't settle for mediocrity, dare to go for more. If you don't dare to seek for development in a childish way, you are in danger of stagnation. This indicates a situation where you become stuck, clinging to everything that is seemingly safe and secure, trying to avoid failures at any cost. Fortunately or unfortunately, failures tend to pick out those that hide from them. The brave ones that bravely and childishly face life and have a creative attitude find a way of tricking the misfortunes in their way.

Nobody has ever achieved anything big by being stuck in their daily routine and without trying something new. If a person does not dare to test themselves in totally unexpected situations, they cannot achieve anything important either. As Einstein said, "Insanity is doing the same thing over and over again and expecting different results." Unfortunately, this is exactly what most grown-ups do day after day.

People tend to their daily errands without daring to try something new, and at the same time they secretly hope to achieve better results. In order for life to offer something to you, you need to be brave enough to try new things. The prize that life will award you with in the end may be a life-changing breakthrough in a grand project or even a few hours of good mood and a pinch of excitement provided by a new hobby.

Children are intuitively seeking new opportunities of development to try new and exciting things. Grown-ups tend to stagnate. They don't dare to give in to their inner drive that pushes them to develop and test their boundaries. If you wish to be truly happy and successful, you will need to follow that drive, just as children do.

A STORY ABOUT CHILDLIKE DEVELOPMENT

—
J. K. Rowling

The year 1993 was the hardest in the life of Joanne Rowling. She has said that she hit rock bottom back then. Sometime before, her mother had passed away; she had divorced her husband and was left alone with her daughter. She was an unemployed single mother who suffered from poverty and depression and, in her own words, felt like a total failure.

Not the best period in life for completely dedicating yourself to writing a book, is it? But Rowling says that this rock bottom gave her the solid ground to build her life on. Misfortune drove her so far that she decided to eliminate everything insignificant from her life. She gave up pretending to be something she wasn't and invested all her energy in just one activity – finishing *Harry Potter and the Philosopher's Stone*.

Three years earlier, trapped in a Manchester-London train, she suddenly got an idea of a lean 11-year-old boy with black hair that isn't aware of his wizard abilities. The idea kept stirring in her mind while she was sitting on the train. Unfortunately, she didn't have a pen to put all the thoughts down right then and there. She

"IT IS OUR CHOICES...
THAT SHOW WHAT
WE TRULY ARE,
FAR MORE THAN
OUR ABILITIES."
–
Joanne Rowling

was also too shy to ask other passengers for a pen. In any case, she had been writing the book for the three successive years with ups and downs. But now, having hit rock bottom and feeling like a total failure, she decided that she was going to devote herself completely to writing and finish her work.

Rowling loved writing. She had written her first story at the age of six. Later, she wrote several short stories for adults, but didn't finish any of them. The Harry Potter idea was so special, however, that Rowling felt like she just had to finish the book. It became the first one she ever finished.

Several publishers declined the Harry Potter manuscript. In the end, the Bloomsbury publishing house agreed to publish her book. Making the advance payment, the publisher recommended Rowling to get a steady job as well, because writers of children's books don't survive on author's fees. Rowling ignored the advice and immediately started working on the second part of *Harry Potter* when she received the advance payment. She had a vision of a series of seven books.

In June 1997, when the book was finally published, it became an instant favorite of both children and many adults. This launched Rowling's global success as a writer. Writing was actually the only type of work Rowling had ever really wanted to do – now she could commit herself to that.

The Forbes magazine currently estimates Joanne Rowling's assets at over a billion dollars. That makes Rowling the only person in the world who has become a billionaire by writing books. Rowling did not stagnate like an adult would have in the toughest period of her life. On the contrary – she dedicated herself illogically and childishly to making her dreams come true. She had constantly developed throughout her life, until she became brave enough and realized all of her potential by writing the Harry Potter series.

She could have easily found typical adult excuses like "I can't make my dreams come true since I need to earn a living for myself and my daughter", "I would make my dreams come true, but I must find a husband first", "I would make my dreams come true, but I must devote myself to my daughter at the moment" etc. These are all empty excuses.

All children actually love happy parents. Happy parents have much more to give to their children than those that "devote themselves to their children", so to speak. If Rowling had made adult excuses for not developing her writing skills, she probably would still be an unhappy single mother struggling with depression and poverty.

GROWN-UPS FEEL REGRET, CHILDREN ENJOY LIFE

Grown-ups have a brilliant mind – it can find a million reasons for regretting and not even a single reason for enjoying life. An adult may regret all sorts of things, for example not giving their best, for making mistakes in the past, for buggering up an opportunity, for not finding the right solution, for working too much or too little. The options are countless.

The human mind is resourceful. It can find ways for feeling regret over events that haven't even happened yet. From early on, grown-ups can feel regret for not achieving their goals, even if they haven't even started striving towards the goal yet. Children don't have these problems. They can't construct thoughts as complicated as that. They just live here and now and enjoy life.

Feeling regret evokes negative thought patterns and emotions – it is as if you are deprived of something. Kids focus their attention on taking chances and enjoying life. Their thoughts follow simple paths and they are unable to analyze things from such a negative perspective.

If you wish to be happy, you need to learn to enjoy life like a child. If you are having a lousy day and things don't go smoothly, then instead of feeling regret and seeking solutions to issues at any cost, take a time out for a bit. Concentrate on enjoying your life, just like children do. Start playing. Think about what you like to do. Going to the beach? Then go there. Or have a walk in the woods. Do sports. Have a chat with a friend at the café. Go shopping and buy something memorable. In a nutshell, award yourself and enjoy life. There are endless opportunities for doing so.

If you are focused on enjoying life and stop feeling regret, solutions will come to you. Just find a way to replace your grown-up attitude with childishness. Being childish, you are creative, mentally free and ready to find resourceful and simple solutions to complex problems. While enjoying your life, you may discover that your problem was a result of grown-up attitude and in reality, there was never a real issue. Taking a goal that is not in tune with reality and is clearly unachievable, it is silly to feel regret if the goal remains unachieved. The problem was in the goal you set for yourself, not

you not being willing or able to achieve it. However, you can only reach that conclusion when you enjoy life like a child, not while being regretful like a grown-up.

The childlike attitude is much more objective. I would go even further and say that enjoying life should be a responsibility one must never fail to meet. What else could be the meaning of life, if not enjoyment? Only a grown-up would be able to prove that feeling regret is more useful than enjoying it.

The brilliant mind of grown-ups can find numerous reasons for regret. Children think simply and don't bother themselves with feeling regret – they enjoy life. If you want to be happy, you need to start enjoying life in a childish way. Trust the process of enjoying life and solutions to your problems will reach you sooner or later.

A STORY ABOUT ENJOYING LIFE LIKE A CHILD
—
Johnny Depp

If you have seen the movie *Pirates of the Caribbean: The Curse of the Black Pearl* or its sequels, you wouldn't be able to imagine the movie without the eccentric pirate captain played by Johnny Depp. The birth of Captain Jack Sparrow's character wasn't as smooth as one might imagine. At the time when the movie company had just started filming *Pirates of the Caribbean*, Disney's management was almost going to fire Depp. As Depp himself said later, "They couldn't understand what I was doing. You know? To the point where Disney wanted to – wanted to fire me. They didn't understand the character. They were actually contemplating subtitling the film."

Disney wanted to fire Depp because the captain he played was arrogant and dissolute, and the movie company was bewildered by such a bizarre character. They were afraid that the role of an alcoholic eccentric captain would bring down the large-budget project. But Depp stood his ground showed Disney its place, telling one of the movie company managers, "You're right, you should fire me – but you'll have to pay me for my time."

"I THINK
THE THING
TO DO IS
ENJOY THE
RIDE WHILE
YOU'RE
ON IT."
—
*John Christopher
Depp II*

Depp had been enjoying life and following his gut feeling in a childish way since his early youth. Back in school, he started a band and dropped out from high school – he was leading a wild life. In the name of his dream, he was staying in his friend's 1967 Chevy Impala for several months and sold pens at a telemarketing company with his band members to earn a living. He then changed his musical career for that of an actor, but there was still a rock star inside him looking to break free.

The role of Jack Sparrow is actually based on Johnny Depp's good personal friend and idol, rock star Keith Richards, the guitarist of the Rolling Stones. By the way, Keith Richards plays Jack Sparrow's father in *Pirates of the Caribbean*. In the end, after some doubts, the Disney management took the risk and trusted Johnny Depp's vision of the bizarre captain. The risk paid off handsomely.

Today, the *Pirates of the Caribbean* franchise is one of the biggest sources of income for Disney. Johnny Depp is one of the greatest Hollywood icons, making it to the Guinness book of records in 2012 as the highest-paid actor in the world with his 75 million dollar annual income.

Depp wasn't thinking about avoiding mistakes when he created the character based on an alcoholic rock star, but about enjoying his role in a childish way. He was playing his inner rock pirate on the screen. If he had stayed in the adult boundaries, he would never have dared to take risks and present such an eccentric and bizarre character as Captain Jack Sparrow. Depp made his dreams come true because he enjoyed life like a child.

GROWN-UPS ARE INFALLIBLE, CHILDREN MAKE MISTAKES

Grown-ups are increasingly more active, educated and infallible. The adults' objective is to be almighty. Making mistakes is not in vogue. Infallibility and precision are. But there is one downside to that. Namely, if you try to avoid mistakes, you will never be able to achieve anything remarkable. When trying to create something special, there is always the possibility that you make mistakes.

Those that have created something truly exceptional have definitely experienced several setbacks in the process. Making mistakes and correcting them is the way to arrive at the right conclusions, and create something new and essential. Grown-ups dread making mistakes, but children don't have that problem. Children are allowed to make mistakes. If we told kids that they weren't allowed to make mistakes, it would hinder their development. Then why do we assume it's any different with grown-ups?

Infallible grown-ups are prepared already at school. Curricula require students to be at least average in all subjects. School doesn't accept being super talented, even world class in one subject and not passing another one. You need to pass both subjects

at least on an average level or you will have to retake the course. You cannot fail.

Infallibility is directly linked with insecurity. The more insecure a person is, the more desperately they try to avoid mistakes. By being childlike and confident, you can afford making mistakes because your self-esteem will not be hurt. Think about the doors that would open up if you allowed yourself to make mistakes. When you have a positive attitude towards making mistakes and being fully child- ish, you can try anything. That would give you a chance to achieve something truly exciting.

Those that are not afraid of making mistakes are constantly suppressed because of the fear that fallible people might achieve something. Those that don't dare to make mistakes themselves, in- vest their energy in cautioning others. Don't let yourself be disturbed by such meanies. You can only ever be happy by making mistakes.

How can you be happy if you constantly think about what will happen if you take a wrong turn? This way, it's impossible to pay all your attention on performance and really achieve something. The desperate avoiding of mistakes hinders achievements and enjoying the life.

For example, imagine a top-league soccer player who scores dozens of goals each year. Now, when he misses a strike that would have normally been a definite goal, then what do you think – is there more talk about the tens of successful goals or this single mishap? Life shows that in this situation, he is treated with a big wave of criticism. Fortunately, an experienced top athlete doesn't usually take it to heart, because such judgments and opinions are not objective and a top player constantly faces unconstructive criticism.

Achievers know better than critics and those that haven't achieved much in life that in order to achieve something, one may make mistakes, that mistakes are inevitable. However, it often happens that a young promising athlete who has reached the top level quits their career after making a "mistake". Grown-ups firmly believe in avoiding all kinds of mistakes. If you want to be happy and make your dreams come true, you need to make mistakes, just as children do. This will enable you to enjoy your activity and you performance is flexible like a child's, not stiff like an adult's.

Grown-ups fear making mistakes like fire. Children are permitted to make mistakes. Desperately dreading mistakes, however, makes it impossible to be happy and make your dreams come true. In order to live happily, you must let go of your fear, and start making mistakes in a childish way.

A STORY ABOUT MAKING MISTAKES
LIKE A CHILD

—

Henry Ford

On a beautiful day in 1885, the 23-year-old Henry Ford first saw an internal combustion engine running on petrol and it was love at first sight. Working as a machine operator's apprentice, Ford had encountered all kinds of devices, but they had not created such enthusiasm in him as this new type of engine that worked on its own power.

Ford imagined a new type of horseless carriage – it would be a revolution in transportation. He made it his life goal to become a pioneer in developing such a horseless carriage. Henry Ford worked night shifts at Edison's lighting company and worked on developing the internal combustion engine during the daytime. He established a workshop in the shed in his back yard, and assembled his first working prototype with help from his friends from scrap metal.

The automobile business was a field of ruthless competition, where new start-ups went under every day. Ford's car seemed nice and ran well, but it was too small and incomplete for mass production. So, he started working on his second car, following the principles of mass production. A year later, his second car was finished and turned out to be a true design miracle. It was easy to drive and maintain. All that Ford needed now was enough capital to launch mass production.

It was a scary business to mass-produce cars at the end of 1890s. It required a lot of capital and a complicated corporate structure, taking into account all the parts needed in production. Ford quickly found the perfect sponsor in William H. Murphy, one of the best-known businessmen in Detroit. The new company was called the Detroit Automobile Company and all stakeholders had high expectations. But soon enough, problems emerged.

Car parts arrived from various places; some of them were defective or weren't quite to Ford's taste. Ford tried to improve the design and move closer to his ideal, but the design work took too long and the shareholders started to become restless. In 1901, a year and a half after establishing the company, the Board of Directors decided to shut it down. They had lost faith in Henry Ford.

That was Ford's first major failure. Analyzing his misfortune, Ford concluded that he was focusing too much on consumer's needs when constructing the car. He wanted to give it a second try, starting with a lighter and smaller vehicle. He managed to convince Murphy to give him another chance, which was very rare in the car industry.

Believing in Ford's genius, they established the Henry Ford Company. But from the very beginning, Ford felt pressure from Murphy to make the car ready for production as soon as possible to avoid the issues they had encountered in the previous company. Ford resented that he was disturbed by people that understood nothing about design or the standards that he wished to implement in the industry. Murphy and his men introduced people from outside to check on the operation processes. This was the breaking point. Ford left the company, this time for good.

Every person experienced in the car business wrote Henry Ford off. He had completely failed for two times by then, and nobody would ever have given him a third chance. But to his friends and

"THE ONLY REAL
MISTAKE IS
THE ONE FROM
WHICH WE LEARN
NOTHING."
–
Henry Ford

family, Ford seemed as joyful and childlike as ever. He told everyone that he had received an invaluable lesson. In his opinion, the reason for failure was that people with money intervened in the issues of mechanics and design, and because he wasn't given enough time to correct his mistakes.

He believed in a childish way that he could achieve his goal if there was a sponsor that would grant him total independence. This was not the regular way of doing business in the increasingly bureaucratic America of the time. He had to invent a totally new form of organization that would match his temperament and needs. He needed an efficient team he could trust and that he would have the last say.

As he put it, „I am looking for a lot of men who have an infinite capacity to not know what can't be done." Considering his reputation, securing financial support was pretty much impossible. After several months of searching, however, he crossed paths with the Scottish emigrant Alexander Malcomson who had made a fortune in the coal business. Like Ford, he also possessed a unique mindset and the willingness to take risks. He agreed to finance Ford's latest venture and not intervene in the production process.

Ford developed a new kind of assembly plant that gave him more control over car design and he created a car known as the Model A. The Model A was the lightest car ever made, simple and durable. The goliath of car industry was born. Later on, the company developed the car into the vehicle called the Ford Model T, which in itself was cultural revolution, as ordinary middle-class people could now afford cars (before that, cars were only affordable for wealthy people).

Nobody with an adult frame of mind starts the same venture for the third time, having failed completely in the previous attempts. Ford childishly believed in making mistakes, not trying to avoid mistakes at all costs. Ford, the synonym for failure, became a pioneer in car industry and one of the wealthiest persons in the world thanks to his childlike mind.

GROWN-UPS ARE RESTLESS WITHIN, CHILDREN ARE CALM

Externally, of course, children are restless and grown-ups are calm. Grown-ups remain much more constrained and proper in most situations, whereas children may act in quite an inappropriate way and speak their minds frankly. But if we look beyond the external appearance, we discover that children are the calm ones.

Children wake up in the morning, and then they eat, play and study. They develop, communicate with their parents and live quietly, going about their activities. In the evening, children go to bed and quickly fall asleep, since they typically have no constant pressure, anxiety or stress.

Many grown-ups, however, feel restless inside when they wake up in the morning. It may be caused by problems at work, with family life, friends and acquaintances or material problems – the list is endless. Grown-ups feel great responsibility and anxiety over situations they can't control. Trying to do their best creates inner restlessness at the same time. Grown-ups just can't enjoy their day, because they are disturbed by feelings of anxiety. The source of which is within their mind.

The adult mind constantly analyzes the surrounding world, looking for opportunities to be super effective, trying to do more of everything better and faster. This kind of striving towards efficiency or greed creates unhealthy anxiety and stress. If you want to be really active, you should lower your pace instead. Try to take it easy, just as children do.

Your life will not improve by rushing around with your focus on perfection. People's productivity won't necessarily improve due to how much they do, but due to what they do. In order to understand what needs to be done, one needs to take time and be calm. Only by acting calmly will we reach the right conclusions. With an attitude like this, the person won't be anxious inside, and is therefore truly efficient and able to achieve much more.

At one time or another, after a day of planning and working, we have all felt that very little was actually accomplished. If the same effort had been made with a calm mind, much more would have got done. At the end of the day, you can look back at the things you have achieved with pride and your soul is filled with enjoyable peace. Just as children who have been running around all day playing different games will easily fall asleep, being happy and contented.

A person can be compared to a car. We can't circle the Earth several times without refueling and maintenance. For a person, refueling means breaks, while maintenance signifies switching to another activity where the results don't matter. For example, take a break and go for a walk. When you return to work after breathing fresh air for an hour, you will feel that all the problems that had made you anxious may be solvable or irrelevant. In fact, most of our daily problems are ultimately irrelevant. What truly matters is how big the problem becomes in our mind.

Children do not typically have such issues with alarming thoughts which is why they are much more peaceful inside. If you don't wish to be disturbed internally, start living at a slower pace, just as children do. You will soon me amazed how smooth your life runs, as you begin consciously avoid rushing and not letting anxious thoughts in.

Children move at a peaceful pace and don't feel anxiety, because they are not looking for rational ultimate efficiency as adults are. If you want to keep your inner stress level low, just start living slowly, just as children do.

A STORY ABOUT CHILDLIKE CALM
—
Dalai Lama XIV

Ever since the Middle Ages, the Dalai Lama has acted as the spiritual and political leader of the Tibetan nation. Never before has the role of Dalai Lama as the protector of Tibetans been as significant as during the reign of the 14th Dalai Lama. The Dalai Lama has organized countless conferences, lectures and seminars on the topics of Buddhism and Tibet in the course of his humanitarian work all over the world. He has met many religious and political leaders to explain the situation of Tibetans.

In 1989, he received the Nobel peace prize for his efforts in peacefully freeing Tibet. The 14th Dalai Lama was inaugurated as the highest spiritual authority at the age of 4 and since the age of 15, he has also been the political leader of Tibet. He managed to actually rule for only a few months before the People's Republic of China invaded Tibet. Since then, Tibet has been suffering under Chinese oppression.

Nine years after the Chinese invasion, the Dalai Lama and his closest advisers became suspicious that the Chinese government under Mao Zedong was planning to murder him. Fearing for his

"WE CAN NEVER
OBTAIN PEACE
IN THE OUTER
WORLD UNTIL WE
MAKE PEACE WITH
OURSELVES."
–
Lhamo Dondrub

life, the Dalai Lama escaped to North India with a few thousand followers and established the Tibetan Government in Exile there. By now, he has lived in exile for over 50 years, trying to make Tibet a democratic country and end the violence. So far, his efforts have not been successful, but his actions have been optimistic, peaceful and relentless. He has been followed by constant failure, but he hasn't let that disturb him and he has continued his work strenuously and patiently.

How to survive for more than 50 years without achieving your goals? The secret of remaining joyful and positive in the face of all his misfortune lies in his faith – Dalai Lama is a Buddhist monk. Buddhists are convinced that life is not and can never be perfect. They concentrate on how to cope in an imperfect world. The following example helps to illustrate the Buddhist worldview.

Once upon a time, there lived an old farmer who had toiled in his fields for many years. One day, his horse ran away. When the neighbors heard the news, they came to see him. "Oh, what a pity," they said compassionately.

"Maybe," answered the farmer.

The next morning, the horse returned, bringing along another three wild horses.

"How wonderful!" the neighbors exclaimed.

"Maybe," said the old man.

The next day, his son tried riding one of the wild horses, but fell off and broke his leg. The neighbors again came over to express their condolences.

"Maybe," the farmer responded.

A day later, military officers came to the village to enlist young men to the army. Seeing that the boy's leg was broken, they didn't enlist him. The neighbors congratulated the farmer on how well everything had turned out.

"Maybe," answered the farmer.

GROWN-UPS DON'T WONDER, CHILDREN ARE FULL OF WONDER

Children are full of wonder when there's rainbow outside. Children are full of wonder when there's a snow storm or heavy rain. Children are full of wonder when a plane takes off. Children are full of wonder when the summer is exceptionally hot. Adults don't see the point in wondering about self-evident things. Adults know that rainbows are caused by the sunlight refracting and reflecting in a rain cloud. Adults may explain why a plane is able to take off with numerous physics laws. For children, however, it's simply unbelievably strange that a plane can fly in the air while everything else is bound to stay on the ground.

The rational attitude of adults stops them from enjoying life. When we lose the ability to wonder about the things around us, we also lose a part of our cheerfulness and eagerness. Grown-ups don't wonder, since they are pushing life in a rational frame. I'm not saying that we should abandon all knowledge that we have as grown-ups. I'm saying that we should be above that knowledge and use it only when we need it. We shouldn't become slaves of knowledge – knowledge should be a tool for us.

The hammer, for example, is a nice and useful tool, but if it starts hitting our fingers without our permission, it's no longer a tool but a master. If we let the mind disturb our cheerfulness and enjoyment from wondering, we will turn it into our enemy. Our mind will stop us from comfortably enjoying life. It would be very sad if we had to give up some of our joy de vivre and childishness when we acquire new knowledge. If you quit wondering, you won't have much use for the knowledge you possess. All great inventors in the history have been both extremely childish and able to wonder, as well as very knowledgeable. Professional knowledge accompanied by childish ability to wonder is a combination that allows us to be successful in our specialty.

If we are able to wonder, we can view the world through a child's eyes. It's a completely different outlook on life, because most

grown-ups are extremely rational. If we are able to wonder, we will childishly feel something much greater and unmeasurable, and can create links and find creative solutions. Wondering is directly linked with happiness, because it involves gratitude and humility. By wondering, we almost admit that there is something bigger than ourselves, like the nature, and we respect it by expressing wonder. If we don't wonder, we also don't respect. We just state that a specific phenomenon exists and needs to exist, without wondering about it.

You should let go of feeling superior due to knowledge, and start wondering in a childish way. This way, you can sense the surroundings much more intensively. Your shallow life will become meaningful. Just like when you were a child, when you went to a new city and looked at everything with your mouth agape. You should look at your surroundings the same way as an adult, because then you will see beyond the surface and reach a sort of enlightenment. A world that was previously invisible will open before your eyes.

When a child sees a world-famous pop star, the child wonders. When a grown-up goes to a concert of a world-famous pop star, the adult may just listen to the songs and completely forget how admirable it is that someone has been able to create so wonderful melodies that touch so many people in the world. When you start wondering about it in a childish way, you may start seeing links and opportunities that enable you to fulfill your dreams. Who wouldn't like to be the start of their lives and achieve something life-changing? If you wonder about other people's creation, you will sooner or later be able to achieve something wonderful yourself.

Grown-ups have given up wondering, because they can explain everything with reason. This attitude, however, stops grown-ups from enjoying their lives fully. In order to be happy, we must be able to wonder, just as children do.

A STORY ABOUT CHILDISH WONDERING

—

Isaac Newton

Newton is considered to be the father of physics. Sir Isaac Newton, the scientist and physicist, made the greatest discovery of all times when he came up with the idea of the force of gravity. A well-known legend says that Newton was sitting under an apple tree and an apple fell on his head. In addition to giving him a sore head, the incident also made Newton wonder why did the apple fall towards the ground, and this is how he discovered g-force.

It didn't happen quite like the legend says, but the real events were quite similar to the legend. The legend concentrates on how the apple falls on Newton's head – just to make it funnier. In reality, Newton was sitting on his porch contemplating, drinking tea and observing the apple tree. Newton realized that the apple didn't really fall, but was drawn to the Earth's center. When he started to think on broader terms – about the Moon, Sun, etc. – he understood that all objects in the universe draw all other objects – with the force of gravity – in proportion with the body mass.

William Stukeley recorded Sir Isaac Newton's memoirs after conversing with him on 15 April 1726 in Kensington: "It (the no-

"WHAT WE KNOW IS A DROP, WHAT WE DON'T KNOW IS AN OCEAN."
–
Sir Isaac Newton

tion of gravity) was occasioned by the fall of an apple, as he sat in contemplative mood. Why should that apple always descend perpendicularly to the ground, he thought to himself. Why should it not go sideways or upwards, but constantly to the Earth's centre? Therefore, does this apple fall perpendicularly or towards the centre? If matter thus draws matter; it must be proportion of its quantity. Therefore, the apple draws the Earth, as well as the Earth draws the apple."

Newton could make this brave discovery only with a totally childlike attitude, because no one in the world had ever thought that objects could attract each other. No adult had ever wondered about the reason why things fall down. Newton moved forward and published his theory in the ground-breaking work, *Philosophiae Naturalis Principia Mathematica* (the *Principia*), published in 1687. In this book, Newton published his three laws of motion that regulate and explain why objects move in the way they do. He also introduced his universal law of gravity that explains the behavior of planets in the solar system and the universe in general. According to Newton's law, each body draws another body towards itself with a force that is proportional to the product of the masses of these bodies, and inversely proportional to the quadrate of their distance.

It is enough to say that without Newton's discovery, the humanity's modern understanding of physics and astronomy would have been impossible. Newton sat on his terrace, and instead of stating the facts like an adult, he decided to wonder like a child about why the apple fell down. This way, Newton's childish attitude changed science forever.

By the way, the apple tree that allegedly inspired Newton astonishingly still exists. The tree that has grown for centuries is now owned by the National Trust that is also the owner of Newton's childhood home in Woolsthorpe Manor near Lincolnshire in England.

GROWN-UPS DON'T HAVE ENOUGH, CHILDREN HAVE PLENTY

Children can't be sad long about what they don't have. They rather simply and pragmatically concentrate on what they have at the moment. Grown-ups are smarter and more demanding. They can think up a whole list of things that they don't have at the moment, constantly feeling in need of something.

Grown-ups feel remorse that they're not successful enough at work, that their home isn't big enough, that their children aren't raised well enough, that a colleague is thinner or that they have too little money. People were as if living their whole lives in constant depravation. In children's mind, the game they're playing at the moment is successful and exciting enough and their home big enough. They also don't worry about their weight or savings.

Adults can't stop worrying about things they can't change. If you don't think you look as good as your friend, should you dedicate the rest of your life to worrying about that? Unfortunately, many adults do. There's always someone that is more skillful, prettier, smarter or more successful than you in some respect. It's absolutely impossible to strive for absolute perfection. It just doesn't exist.

There are billions of people in the world, and even if you manage to become the best in something, you can be sure that one day, you will be overthrown. Absolute success is not permanent. Concentrate on activity. Believe that you have enough even if someone has more. Happy and successful people don't strive towards absolute perfection, but accept their inadequacy. Instead of being better than everyone, they childishly believe that they have enough, and try to achieve something unique and inherent to them.

You can only be happy, if you concentrate on what you have at present. Children and childish-minded adults always see a glass half full, while those that think in an adult way see the glass as half empty

and feel regret. If you believe that you have enough, you will find faith and strength to devote to making your dreams come true – that takes a big dose of childish simplicity, and will in turn offer joy and enthusiasm. But if you feel that you don't have enough at the moment, you will always think that way, even in the midst of your numerous accomplishments. You may remain thinking poorly so to say, if you don't change your frame of mind. Whatever you achieve, in your soul you will still feel that you are deprived of something.

The way your life seems to an objective bystander may totally differ from the way you see it yourself. Someone that finds their life to be lacking will always feel that they don't have enough, however meaningful and rich their life may turn out to be.

Recognize that you have enough. Rejoice like a child about what you have and avoid any kind of regret. People thinking in an adult way believe that they will become happy, when they have fulfilled their dreams, and that they are unhappy if they don't. But when their dreams do come true, they won't understand why they didn't become happy. Actually, you need to be childishly happy all the time, not only when an external factor makes you feel happy. The greatest happiness is actually being able to feel fulfillment and gratitude every day for moving towards your dreams. The moving itself is the greatest joy, because there's enough of it for every day, not just one, the day that your dream comes true. This way of thinking, however, is only possible with childish attitude.

Children have enough, they don't feel deprived. Grown-ups, on the other hand, constantly feel that they need more and they don't have enough. In order to be happy, you need to feel childish fulfillment all the time, and concentrate on what you already have, not what you don't yet have.

A STORY ABOUT CHILDISH FULFILMENT

—

Mother Teresa

Mother Teresa has moved beyond her human existence, and become a legend and symbol of charity. Mother Teresa, née Agnes, was born into a wealthy family in Albania. At the age of 8, Agnes experienced great loss when her father died and the whole family suffered from economic difficulties. In this period, Agnes took interest in religion. The future holy sister found her calling as a 12-year-old, and decided to dedicate her life to missionary work.

This kind of a determined choice in such an early age is admirable. She wanted to live her life by serving and helping others. She believed that the church provided an opportunity to do that, and she decided to take service as far as possible. At the age of 18, she became a catholic nun, and she was initiated as Teresa. She decided to do everything in her power as a nun to help those in need. She didn't waste time on constantly thinking how many resources were absent; instead, she childishly concentrated on what was in her power at that moment.

However bizarre or insignificant a good deed seemed, Mother Teresa still carried it out enthusiastically. For example, she once

"IF YOU CAN'T FEED A HUNDRED PEOPLE, THEN FEED JUST ONE."

–

Anjezë Gonxhe Bojaxhiu

travelled through a war zone, risking her life to save 37 children from the front line. When she was flying on a plane, she used to ask the cabin crew to collect the food leftovers. She used that food to feed the poor and hungry.

When Teresa was 36, she felt God's call to go and help the poor people in India. In 1929, she arrived in India with the Loreto sisters as a missionary. To help and feed the poorest, she starved herself as well. She even went so far that in the end, she had to beg for her own food. As she once told Princess Diana, "To heal other people you must suffer yourself."

Mother Teresa started from pure enthusiasm and did everything in her power, and although it may have seemed silly to bystanders first off, her efforts soon started bearing fruit. The state and church leaders noticed her activity and aid for the poor started flooding in. But Mother Teresa remained faithful to her mission and values.

For example, when she had already become famous and Pope Paul VI wished to meet her during a visit to India, Mother Teresa declared that she was too busy with her work – meeting the poor. The Pope was impressed by her devotion and he declared his obligation to help her. The Pope gave her his Lincoln that he had used on his state visit. Mother Teresa accepted the present and then sold it at an auction to raise funds for helping people. Some time later, the Pope managed to meet Teresa, but her attitude remained the same.

She didn't believe in an adult way that in order to help the poor, hungry and abandoned, one needs a lot of money or power. She didn't believe in the power-worship, but was childishly convinced that she just had to do as much she could at that particular moment, and respecting the needs of the needy is more important than honoring power.

In 1979, Mother Teresa received the Nobel peace prize. As a surprise to the organizers, she refused to participate in the traditional reception and festivities. Mother Teresa asked instead that the 192,000 dollar budget would be donated towards helping the poor that she worked and lived with. Her Nobel Prize donation fed close to 15,000 hungry people. Since Mother Teresa felt childish fulfillment from doing the simplest good deeds and always gave as much as she had at that particular moment, she helped thousands of poor people with her childish attitude and set an example to many do-gooders today.

When Mother Teresa as an internationally famous benefactor was once asked how to improve world peace, she answered, "Go home and love your family." Yes, in order to promote world peace, one doesn't need big means and lots of power. One simply needs childish attitude that says that you are not lacking the means – in fact, you already have enough to help others.

GROWN-UPS' LIFE IS COMPLICATED, CHILDREN'S LIFE IS SIMPLE

Grown-ups like to live life more complicated than it really is. Children see life as simple. The truth is that life is actually simple and we shouldn't think it more complicated. It's always possible to choose what to do with your life; no one else can decide it for you.

If you meet a completely miserable person, ask them what the problem is. They may answer that they don't like their job that they are forced to do, since it poisons their life, making them miserable. But they can't quit either, because they have a mortgage and the family has certain expectations regarding their income. A childish person would answer that they should forget about that job and start doing something they enjoy more. Move to a smaller space and their family will understand.

Every real family understands that a person can't be miserable on a daily basis only to pay big bills. But wise adults that don't see their lives in a simple way may start explaining in a long, well-reasoned and logical manner, why their lives are so complicated. That kind of person presents convincing arguments why they simply can't quit their lousy job and why they need to earn more money

than they would make with work they'd really enjoy. Don't believe them. No child would.

The size of the home isn't so important as to replace it for personal happiness. If home size did matter, the person wouldn't be unhappy, but would do their well-paid and unpleasant work with joy. But the truth is that in this case, the end doesn't justify the means. Activity provides more enjoyment than the end goal. Adults, however, make career choices only by studying facts, not trusting their emotion. In fact, they should just trust their gut instinct. If something makes a person unhappy, he or she shouldn't continue the activity, because there is always a solution.

Life is actually simple, not complicated – we need to see it that way ourselves. Don't be misguided by the details, because they may distract your attention from simplicity. We should concentrate on the bigger picture. The wiser grown-ups become, the bigger is the danger that they may not be able to distinguish important from insignificant.

Take people that have gambled off all of their money and that of their close ones at the casino. They aren't necessarily simple-minded

people with no education. Educated and economically secure people may also take their money to the casino. They may be top specialists, managers or company owners. If a wealthy person gets addicted to gambling, they pull under their beloved ones as well, because they're trusted and have access to great sums of money.

Any child could understand that in reality, the casino always wins and the player only gets enjoyment from playing. It's just a matter of time when the person loses everything. If the people that gamble their money away at the casino have an adult attitude, they believe they can trick life. What other explanation is there to the fact that, for example, a CFO whose specialty is to plan cash flow doesn't understand that a casino is not the place for increase one's assets. It's not a question of small wisdom but a question of the person's attitude. They can't see life clearly anymore. Life is not in itself complicated but easy.

There are still many grown-ups who still ignore that simple truth. They underestimate the laws of life and believe that they are wise enough to trick life. They continue to get entangled in problems, because they don't believe in simplicity of life. They think that life is complicated and as adults, they can trick life. They're wrong – life is actually simple.

Grown-ups think that life is complicated and that they can trick life.
Actually, the principles of life are easy, and we have a much better chance at applying them successfully in our advance with a childish attitude.

A STORY ABOUT CHILDISHLY SIMPLE LIVING
—
Steve Jobs

Steve Jobs was the co-founder of Apple Computers, an innovator, a cult businessman and a multimillionaire. By Jobs' initiative, Apple pioneered several technological revolutions, including the iPhone and iPad. In 2005, in a speech he gave to the graduates of the Stanford University, Steve Jobs talked about him dropping out of college and why he considers it one of the best decisions of his life.

The pressure to go to college started before Steve Jobs was even born. His biological mother was a young and single senior student who decided to give her child up for adoption. Steve's mother was strongly convinced that her son should be adopted by college graduates – that settled everything and little Steve was to be adopted by a lawyer and his wife. At the last moment, when little Steve Jobs had just been born, the foster family decided that they wanted to adopt a girl instead.

Thus, Steve Jobs' eventual parents, then next on the waiting list, received an unexpected call in the middle of the night, asking, "We have an unexpected baby boy; do you want him?" Parents said, "Of

"REMEMBERING THAT YOU ARE GOING TO DIE IS THE BEST WAY I KNOW TO AVOID THE TRAP OF THINKING YOU HAVE SOMETHING TO LOSE. YOU ARE ALREADY NAKED. THERE IS NO REASON NOT TO FOLLOW YOUR HEART."

–

Steven Paul Jobs

course." But when Steve Jobs' biological mother discovered that the mother planning to adopt had never graduated from college and the father had not even finished high school, she refused to sign the final adoption papers. She relented only a few months later when the perspective parents made a promise that he would go to college someday.

Steve Jobs went to college 17 years later. Naively, he picked a college that is as expensive as Stanford, meaning that all the money that his working class parents could save up over their lives was spent on their son's tuition. After six months of college, Job didn't see its value. He had no idea what he wanted to do with his life and how college should help him figure that out.

Instead of keeping spending his parents' savings, he decided to drop out and believed that everything would fall into place. Back then, it was scary for Steve Jobs, but looking back, he considered it one of the best decisions of his life. He trusted his gut feeling and childishly decided in the favor of simple living.

Having dropped out from college, he could abandon the obligatory courses that didn't interest him, and listen to the ones that really offered him something. Steve Jobs didn't have his own dorm room, so he slept on the floor in his friends' rooms, and collected coke bottles worth a 5-cent deposit. He walked seven miles every Sunday evening to get a decent meal at the Hare Krishna temple. Steve Jobs enjoyed that childish simplicity in his life.

Many things he stumbled upon back then with his curiosity and intuition turned out to be invaluable later on. For example, the Reed College provided the best calligraphy training in the whole country. Every poster and label in the campus was written in a beautiful handwriting. Since Steve Jobs had decided in the favor of simple living and he didn't have to participate in the obligatory lessons, he decided to learn calligraphy. He learnt different fonts and how to vary their spacing. He learnt the factor that makes good writing style a great one.

Steve Jobs was enthralled by calligraphy. Years later, he recounted: "It was beautiful, historical, artistically subtle in a way that science can't capture, and I found it fascinating." There was no chance that he could ever apply it in his life. But ten years later, when Steve Jobs was planning his first Macintosh computer, he remembered the calligraphy skills he had once learned. The Mac became the first computer with beautiful typography. Steve Jobs said that if he had not stumbled upon that specific course, Mac would have never had tens of font styles or fonts with proportional spaces. And since Windows copied them off Mac, it's likely that no personal computer would have had them. If Jobs hadn't dropped out from college and hadn't gone to the calligraphy class as a result, the modern day computers wouldn't have such a beautiful typography.

It's of course only one tiny example of how simple living pays off in the long run. We could endlessly continue telling such stories from Steve Jobs' life. As Steve Jobs put it himself, "Of course it was impossible to connect the dots looking forward when I was in college. But it was very, very clear looking backwards ten years later." Just as he saw looking back that dropping out from college was useful for him in the end, although it was impossible to predict in the beginning. Living simply like a child means trusting yourself, your fate and the bright future.

If Steve Jobs had been afraid of making the right decision as an adult is, and hadn't dared to drop out, he would probably have never changed world history and made the great contribution in the development of personal computers and smart devices.

GROWN-UPS MAKE PLANS, CHILDREN ACT

Like the old saying goes, life passes by while you make plans for it. If you ask a really old person whose days are running out what they regret about their lives, it is likely that they regret spending too much time on making plans and too little time on acting and enjoying life. Instead of planning, they could have lived whole-heartedly.

As children, we were active. When we felt the urge to do something, we acted upon it. We didn't waste much time on planning. When people grow up, they tend to plan activities instead of acting. Planning is a good way of postponing the act itself. For example, if we don't dare to undertake what we'd really like to do, it's comfortable to hide behind planning, consoling ourselves that we are still thinking, it's not time for acting yet.

There are no such people that live the life of their dreams, constantly making plans at the same time. For a satisfied person, the relationship between planning and acting has tilted towards the latter. Making plans, you can be happy for a short time. Making lofty plans, you can raise sky high in your thoughts, making big air castles. However, at the moment, you need to start acting, you

suddenly lose heart and become afraid of your utopian goals. You feel as if you're paralyzed. You wake up from your dreams into the reality. It happened, because you planned too much.

Grown-ups love planning. We make five-year plans or write down promises for the next year on the New Year's Eve. We write down our goals – how much we'd like to weigh, how much money should we have in a year, what kind of people we would like around us. When the year goes by, we again discover being unsatisfied and that our goals haven't been fulfilled. Why? Because, we paid too much attention on planning and too little on acting.

If we write down that in a year, we would like to weigh 20 pounds less, it's relatively certain that we won't meet that objective. But if we set the goal of losing 6 pounds and try achieving it in two months, it's quite realistic that we are able to lose 20 pounds in a year. We just need to act steadily, as children do, without making big plans, as grown-ups tend to do.

It seems that adults don't like small realistic achievements, because they mainly set great goals. Children first act and then think.

Actually, adults should do some acting first, and only then adjust their plan during the activity, continuing to act right away. Not everything can be foreseen beforehand. Planning should be done hand in hand with action.

Children do whatever comes to their mind. No child would dream of making plans all day about going outside with a friend to play. The child just tells his or her parents, "I want to go outside to play!" End of story. Meeting up with a friend, they immediately find something exciting to play. We, adults, should learn that attitude from children.

Don't be someone that waits until all lights turn green before starting acting. All lights will never turn green! Otherwise, you will wait forever for conditions to become favorable and all answers known. In order to enjoy life and be happy, we must be much braver and consider the outcomes less.

Discover the childish magic of the moment for yourself! If you have a plan you could fulfill, however, stop planning and realize the idea. In reality, doing the brave and exciting things our intuition finds right may not always turn out the way we initially thought, but in some magic way, something completely different and maybe even better happens. If you act in a childish way and give up the endless planning, good opportunities will cross your path. But if you decide for the adult-like planning, you can rest assured that nothing will ever happen. Sitting behind your desk and planning must be very safe – nothing happens. But if you go on an adventure in a childish way, step outside and see what life has in store for you, things start happening.

Planning *per se* is definitely necessary, but it should be done during action, because then, life can give you feedback and you can change your plans on the go. I know many adults who are planners through and through. You probably know someone whose talk of their future plans of actions sound wonderful. They may even make you jealous with their great and ideal plans. Measure them by their actions.

People that act on an impulse like a child may not tell others about their plans. They know that they can't present a precise plan, as it might change during action. The veteran planners mistakenly think that childish actors just stumble across lucky chances. No, they just value planning less than acting.

Give up being an adult-like planner. Start acting on the heat of the moment as children do, and you will soon discover the magic of the moment that will lead you to far better results than you could have ever planned! If you really take part in life, you will act on an impulse.

A STORY ABOUT CHILDISHLY TAKING ACTION
—
Winston Churchill

To move to politics successfully, one needs political capital. In other words, one has to become famous for something and win people's trust. The story of Winston Churchill's becoming a politician is quite an adventure.

His youth was definitely the most exciting and dangerous of that of all British prime ministers. When the young Churchill was 24 years old, he started working as a war correspondent with the conservative daily newspaper Morning Post after leaving army service. Soon, he was sent to South Africa to report on the Boer Wars between the British and Dutch colonialists.

However, the enemy imprisoned him when the armored train was ambushed. Churchill was transported to a jail called State Model Schools in Pretoria along with the other prisoners. But the future head of state did not despair. Since the beginning of his imprisonment, he carefully observed the guards' daily routine and soon discovered a time gap in their watch where none of the guards watched the prison wall. After a few weeks of captivity, he decided to take his chances at night and escape.

"IT IS ALWAYS
WISE TO LOOK
AHEAD,
BUT DIFFICULT
TO LOOK
FURTHER THAN
YOU CAN SEE."
–
*Winston Leonard
Spencer-Churchill*

But he had some scores to settle before running away. The gentleman that he was, he paid his debts to a Boer shopkeeper that had sold him tobacco, and he also wrote an expression of gratitude to the Boer war minister who had been helpful towards him. Then, he escaped over the wall and hid himself in a nearby villa until he was able to jump on a passing train. He hid himself between coal sacks on the freight train until sunrise and at dawn, continued his escape on foot. He walked along the railway for days, slept in ditches and stole food wherever he could. He searched garbage cans for newspapers to get information about the manhunt organized to capture him.

There was a bounty of £25 on him. In the end, exhausted and desperate from thirst and hunger, he knocked on a door in a mining village. By a stupidly lucky chance, the door was opened by Sir John Howard, leader of the Transvaal Collieries. After answering the door, Howard responded to Churchill's plea, "Thank God you have come here! It is the only house for twenty miles where you would not have been handed over. But we are all British here, and we will see you through."

Mr. Howard initially hid the fugitive in a coalmine, then squeezed Churchill in a small space on a coach carrying wool balls and transported him to a safe location. When Winston Churchill reached Durban in South Africa, he became a hero. His wonderful prison break raised him to the status of a hero back home in England.

Winston Churchill was a childish actor. He escaped from jail without any specific plan, but his tenacity, belief and childish action lead him to freedom in the end. If Churchill had made plans in an adult way, he would probably still be waiting for his release from the Pretoria jail. Thanks to acting in a completely childish way, the public saw him as a hero, which later enabled him to become one of the most influential politicians in the world.

GROWN-UPS CARE ABOUT THE RESULT, CHILDREN CARE ABOUT THE ACTIVITY

For grown-ups, success means achieving better results in something than others do. Are people who have met their objectives and are considered successful, happy? Yes and no. I believe that there are about as many happy people among successful people as there are among the unsuccessful or just a bit more. In any case, it can't be said that success in a specific profession will definitely make you happy. Many adult-like achievers still feel empty and unsuccessful in their souls after meeting their high objectives.

True success, the kind that will definitely make you happy, presumes that you childishly enjoy the activity with which you wish to achieve success. If you have set the right goals that allow you to enjoy the whole ride, you will feel successful and happy throughout the time you strive towards the goals, long before achieving them. If you really enjoy the ride in a childish way, the likelihood that you will reach your goal, will increase. And when you have reached the goal, it's not a big deal anymore, because you won't need the result to be happy. You are happy all the time as it is. Instead, you will set new objectives to reach.

We will never achieve truly brilliant results in something if we don't enjoy the activity completely. Have you noticed that there is a pattern in life that if you want something too much, you won't get it? At the same time, when you are simply childishly playful, you reach your goal without much effort. This obstinate wanting comes from fixating on the result, not on enjoying the activity. Children enjoy their activity, because they don't set out to achieve. They have a much wiser attitude towards tasks – based on what they like to do. Their indirect goal is reached as if in passing.

Grown-ups, however, like to leave a successful impression of themselves, even if they don't like what they are doing, and aren't very successful at all. Don't be fooled by that. Pretending to be successful is easy, we just need to let everyone know that we are busy, and involve ourselves in all kinds of activities, so we look needed and engaged.

People take bank loans to buy an expensive car. Next, they take a mortgage and buy as fancy a house as they can. Now, all you need to do is constantly pretend as if it's a piece of cake and people will start believing that they are seeing a successful grown-up. But there's something missing. You can fool everyone else, but not the person that faces you in the mirror each morning. Your gut feeling will tell you, if you are truly successful, or just pretend to be.

The most important component of true success is to do something that you really like. Be like a child and do what you really enjoy, not what you are made to do by a norm or a trend. Grown-ups are so blinded by results that they can't see beyond them. Therefore,

they pick a profession by results. I dare say that all people that have based their career choices on results alone are actually unhappy inside. A result is a short-term motivation.

Children know that one can only be happy by enjoying each moment. The result won't compensate all the passionless moments. I'm not saying that if you do what you enjoy, you will accomplish everything without effort. It's still hard, but exciting at the same time, because it captivates your soul and senses, not only your mind. Pick a job that you truly enjoy and you'll be able to enjoy your activities, as a child enjoys his or her favorite game.

We should only set the kind of goals towards which we enjoy striving. Exactly as children choose games according to liking and make new achievements in the process. Doing so, you will begin truly enjoying your work, and will be happy.

A STORY ABOUT CHILDISH CONCENTRATION ON THE ACTIVITY

—

Michael Jordan

Michael Jordan was not born as the best. Jordan's story is actually a typical case of an ugly duckling. Although he loved basketball more than anything, he lacked natural talent and height at school. Michael's elder brother Larry was the most talented basketball player of the Jordan family in his youth, and Michael's main opponent.

Larry was taller and stronger, and beat the smaller Michael in all one-on-one games they played. Michael was depressed by constantly losing to his brother, but he was also incredibly competitive, which meant that losing motivated him to practice even more to beat Larry. Michael enjoyed the competitive aspect of basketball more than anything. He wasn't considering the result in the long perspective as much as playing and competing in a given moment.

When Michael was 15, he had reached five foot eight and was now a whole two inches taller than his brother. Since he had done so much work to not be beaten by his brother while being shorter, he was now able to turn the tables on him. By the way, despite not losing to his brother anymore, Larry was still such an example to

Michael back then that he picked the number 23 as his shirt number when he became world famous namely because of him.

Since Larry played under number 45 and Michael couldn't pick that, he divided 45 by two and rounded it up, getting 23. When Jordan had played for a year in the Laney High School juniors' team, the high school's main team was looking for extra players for the upcoming play-offs. Michael and his best friend Leroy Smith decided to apply. Mike was convinced he would be picked.

Although Michael had practiced hard, and developed into a masterful player, the much taller Leroy was picked in the team instead. It was a great disappointment and a turning point in Michael's career. He swore that he would never let something like that happen again, and dedicated himself to becoming as good a basketball player he could get.

Ruby Sutton, Jordan's PE teacher from Laney High School, has said that at the time, when she came to open the gym between 7 and 7.30 in the morning, she could always hear a ball bouncing, whether it was fall, wintertime or summertime. Michael was always there practicing early in the morning. He didn't waste time or think about results in an adult way, but just trusted his instincts and practiced away. He completely concentrated on playing, like a child.

"JUST PLAY.
HAVE FUN.
ENJOY THE GAME."
–
Michael Jeffrey Jordan

Fortunately, nature stepped in to help him out, and he grew six inches taller over the summer. No one could have predicted this, but if he hadn't practiced while being short with such dedication, he would never have turned out such a good basketball player. Life awards those that act and love their work.

By the way, some scientists believe that the constant stretches and jumps, e.g. towards the basket, as a teenager may favor growing tall. In any case, the six inches taller and skillful Jordan became the full member of a college basketball team, giving him the chance to shine.

In 1984, Jordan joined Chicago Bulls, being the third pick for the team in that season. The first cup title came seven years later. Altogether, Michael won six NBA cup titles and two Olympic gold medals over his career, and most experts consider him the best basketball player of all times.

Jordan's playing is characterized by gracefulness and style. The extensive and graceful flights through the air; the relentless defense play; the technically intricate dribbling and throws. He played in a creative and joyful way like a child. It seemed that he was not worried about the final result. Namely that kind of attitude, concentrating on playing, not the result, enabled Jordan to score more last minute points than any other basketball player in history.

GROWN-UPS BLEND IN, CHILDREN STAY THEMSELVES

Grown-ups desperately wish to blend in because they're afraid of being wrong. They are afraid of becoming the laughing stock of others. The fashion industry of the whole world would struggle if people wouldn't try to wear whatever is declared "right" at the moment.

Grown-ups spend much energy on doing what other people consider to be right. Children do exactly what their heart desires. Children don't think about what might be popular. If they are attracted to an activity, they will do precisely that. An adult who only follows other people's opinions will never become the person they could have become – a true personality who is sincerely happy and can do what they really want to do. If you want to be happy, you must stay yourself like a child.

Instead of thinking about what others think, start thinking about what you think. You don't need to buy the bestselling car of the moment. This doesn't apply, of course, if it happens to be exactly the car you desire. But many people buy a more popular car only to be like others.

With this attitude, we give away a piece of ourselves only to gain approval from the society. Grown-ups that behave like that just can't resist the salesman's argument that it's the bestseller so it must be good!

The reason why grown-ups aren't happy is namely because when trying to do what others find right, they neglect what they themselves find right. People give up their dreams because of other people's approval. Sense in a childish way, what you really want, and be brave in achieving it. Forget about other people's approval and start living as yourself in a childish way! Many adults live to an old age and only find out as an elderly person that they have sought someone else's approval their whole lives, instead of following their heart.

Don't be one of them! Become yourself today. In fact, people respect those that have their own opinion and aren't trying to copy someone else or live someone else's life. Those that don't wish to be like others are teased at first, trying to make people with different

opinion or personality like themselves. But if you stick to your principles and aren't desperate about becoming part of the mass, you will be convincing in the end, and your individuality will be respected. You will become a person that is respected for what you are, and others won't presume anymore that you are like everybody else.

Then, figuratively speaking, you can be the master of your life. However, that kind of life is only available to childlike people!

If you give up seeking approval in an adult way and remain yourself in a childlike manner, many doors that were closed will open before you. You will become the person you truly wish to become inside, and others won't presume anymore that you do everything by their example. They will respect your individuality.

A STORY ABOUT CHILDISHLY
REMAINING YOURSELF

—

Bill Gates

When Bill Gates, the future founder of Microsoft and the wealthiest person in the world, was still in high school, he and his friend Allen polished their programming skills at a local computer company called C-Cubed. Since they were only students, they didn't have access to the kind of information that the full-time workers did. And this frustrated them.

Thus, Bill and Allen decided to go hunting for information one night. To do so, they dove into the company's giant waste containers. Since Allen was taller, he helped the shorter Gates climb up and so he was digging away in the garbage, looking for interesting information. When they managed to dig out the source code of TOPS-10, it revealed many secrets for them, and they were able to shine in their work.

That incident is only a small example of Bill Gates' life before Microsoft. Bill Gates' attitude was childlike – he wasn't bothered by the established norms and rules. He decided to stay himself in a childish way and do things that people with an adult attitude would never do. For example, go digging in a company's waste container

"I'M A GEEK."
–
William Henry Gates III

to seek for information. Bill and Allen didn't want to blend in; instead, they childishly invented their own way of how to strive on.

With that childlike attitude, Gates later established a unique company that developed the Windows95 operating system and made Gates the wealthiest person in the world. Gates isn't ashamed of staying himself, and daringly admits being a geek.

GROWN-UPS ARE SERIOUS, CHILDREN LAUGH

Grown-ups prefer being serious. It looks reasonable. Abundant laughing, on the other hand, may seem too frivolous. Adults want to be credible. If we try to act accordingly and have the respective mentality, it will start damaging our health sooner or later.

Scientists have researched that phenomenon for a long time, and found that the more laughter there is in a person's life, the healthier they are; it also increases our life quality and happiness. Children love laughing – with and without reason. If you wish to experience happiness and fulfill your dreams, you must learn how to laugh from children. The more you laugh, the better!

You can also deceive yourself with laughter. Try it when you are in a bad mood. Smile! In the beginning, just smirk. Then go on to laughing and in the end, laugh till you roar with laughter. When you find even a smallest reason to make yourself laugh, you will soon notice that the bad mood disappears and the solution to your problems is right in front of you. As the saying goes, "If you're too busy to laugh, you are too busy."

Grown-ups have learnt how to pretend laughing instead of laughing. Children laugh sincerely and from the bottom of their hearts. They laugh when there is something to laugh about and if there's nothing funny, they don't laugh. But grown-ups often act in the opposite way. If there is a funny situation, they hold back because they're unsure if it's appropriate to express their joy in the given moment. They're worried of how it seems to others. At the same time, if they need to make small talk in a circle of people, they laugh uncontrollably, all the time. But that laughter is fake – the mouth laughs, but not the eyes or the heart. This kind of laughter is rather harmful than healthy, because we are as if living a couple of centimeters outside our bodies. The natural self is not in the foreground; we merely try to blend in and please others.

Successful and happy people know that in order to really be liked, we need to be ourselves in the deepest sense of the word. We need to be sincere and express the emotions we actually feel. Only in this manner – sincerely and showing our true emotions, as children do, will we earn other people's respect. Only by sincerely laughing and being sincerely sad, can we be truly happy. Surround yourself with people that you laugh with often and uncontrollably; with those that allow you to let go completely and childishly. Organize your life in a way that you have a reason to laugh, because then you have a wholesome life.

Instead of laughing, grown-ups have learnt how to pretend laughing in an appropriate moment. Children laugh sincerely and wholeheartedly. Only by laughing from the bottom of our heart can we be truly happy.

A STORY ABOUT CHILDISH LAUGHING
—
the laughing Buddha

Laughing Buddha statues can be found in people's homes, workplaces, restaurants and temples all around the world. People have believed for centuries that the fat laughing Buddha statue brings good fortune to them and their business. Just a glance at the statue is said to instill feelings of imminent good luck and good will. In the western world, it's often believed that it's a statue of Siddharta Gautama Buddha that lived in the 6th century and founded Buddhism. In fact, the laughing Buddha is a Chinese Zen monk who lived in the 10th century.

They are confused with each other because Buddha means an enlightened state of mind, not the name of a specific person. The laughing Buddha's name is Budai in the Chinese tradition and Hotei in the Japanese tradition. Hotei is the god of content and happiness, who is usually depicted with a large stomach and a bulky cloth bag that never gets emptier. The bag symbolizes happiness, good fortune and abundance. The laughing Buddha is also called a wandering monk.

GROWN-UPS ARE SERIOUS, CHILDREN LAUGH

**"IT IS BETTER TO TRAVEL WELL
THAN TO ARRIVE."**
–
Siddharta Gautama Buddha

According to the legend, he travelled from town to town and handed out sweets to all children that gathered around him. He put his bag down, looked in the sky and laughed, even if no one joined him. Soon, his laughter became infectious and someone in the company started laughing whole-heartedly. Being around him, one didn't need a reason for laughing or being happy.

Based on the legends, it seems that the laughing Buddha was just a childish monk that burst laughing without reason, infecting everyone around him with his childish laughter. Now, the childishly laughing statue hopefully lifts the mood of millions of people who have displayed it in their rooms.

GROWN-UPS HAVE RESPONSIBILITIES, CHILDREN HAVE OPPORTUNITIES

Grown-ups are like machines for fulfilling their responsibilities. They wake up in the morning to meet the prescribed norm. They often stick the magic words "I HAVE TO" in front of their sentences. And there we go – *I have to* do this, I *have to* go there. It seems as if the adults don't wish to do all the numerous activities out of free will, but they just *have to* fulfill some responsibilities on a daily basis.

We constantly have a plan that we try to fulfill like slaves. We educate, train and develop ourselves in order to be great and wise on some day and then occupy ourselves with things we HAVE TO do. The smarter and more developed we are, the less we do things we want to do and the more we do things we have to do. The expectations and plans get bigger and bigger.

Instead of responsibilities, children have opportunities. They don't feel they need to do something. They do whatever they see fit at the moment. When they feel like going outside, they go outside to play. When they feel like resting, they lie down for a nap. There's no hurry, no plan to fulfill in panic.

It's amazing that grown-ups that should be the masters of their lives are in fact not in control in many cases. As a grown-up, you should be able to look on life as a choice between endless possibilities. You can do whatever you want because you are a grown-up and no one can forbid you to. If even children have opportunities, why do you only have to have responsibilities?

Begin by saying that you want to do it if there is something you want to start doing, not that you have to do it. The words HAVE TO convey a sense of forced labor, making us feel as if we didn't have the right to decide about our actions.

Maybe grown-ups want to be a bit self-denying and surrender to a greater power, a superior obligation above us, presenting it as an excuse for not enjoying life and being happy. Grown-ups often even apologize for their behavior to their children, saying that they don't have time to play with them because they are obliged to do something else. This is actually a lie, because grown-ups CAN play with their children any time they feel like it. The limits only exist in people's minds.

Some parents never play with their kids due to lack of time. It's physically impossible, of course, that one person has less time than another. The day lasts for 24 hours for everyone; no one is in a privileged status. It's a question of choices. When we say we don't have time, it would be in fact an honest thing to say that we don't wish to take time for it, because another activity is more important to us. It's your own decision. Don't fool yourself, saying you don't have time. Nobody else has the right to decide about your time. Start seeing your life through the prism of endless opportunities instead of responsibilities, just like children do.

Grown-ups should be the masters of their lives, but they are actually not. They just fulfill a prescribed plan from day to day. They have endless responsibilities. But children have endless opportunities. Don't burden yourself with endless responsibilities; start seeing opportunities in your responsibilities and your world view becomes much more childish and positive.

A STORY ABOUT CHILDISHLY SEEING OPPORTUNITIES

—

Charlie Chaplin

Charlie Chaplin was the greatest silent movie actor in the 20th century because of the character of a small tramp he created. Chaplin himself had quite a lot in common with his famous character.

Charlie Chaplin's childhood passed with his half-brother suffering from poverty, hunger and abuse. Since their mother, a variety singer, was often locked in a mental hospital and their drunkard father had abandoned them, they lived in correctional facilities or simply in the streets. Chaplin often had to spend nights out in the open, as is befitting to a tramp.

He started his stage career already at the age of five, filling in for his mother at the Aldershot variety theatre in East London, which was considered the nightmare of entertainers. Most of the variety audience was made up of soldiers who only sought to mock the performers. Chaplin's mother had the tendency to lose her voice for no apparent reason in the middle of her performance from time to time. When it happened, the director used small Charlie as a replacement singer.

Once, Chaplin sang "Jack Jones" that made the audience throw coins on the stage. Charlie stopped singing and announced he would collect the money before continuing. This joke earned him his first burst of laughter. Over time, Chaplin developed into an expert comedian and desiring wealth, he entered the movie business.

The public received Chaplin's first movie with indifference. In 1914, the 24-year-old Chaplin worked at the Keystone movie studio where he had to act in his second movie, *Kid Auto Races at Venice*. On a regular shooting day, the studio boss Mark Sennett told Chaplin to show up on the set in comedy make-up and crack some jokes to spice up the movie. Instead of fulfilling his duty like a good adult, Charlie saw a childish opportunity to make something big happen.

According to Charlie Chaplin, he had an idea on the way to the wardrobe to wear saggy pants, too big shoes, grab a bamboo walking stick and wear a top hat. Chaplin's idea was for everything to be in disagreement: saggy pants, tight coat, small hat and large shoes. In order to make the 24-year-old Chaplin's character look older, he was given a moustache, because it doesn't hide the facial expressions.

Chaplin has said that he had no clue what the nature of his character was supposed to be like. But the moment he had the clothes and make-up up, he started feeling what the character might be like. And by the time he reached the stage, the character had been fully born.

And so IT began – Charlie Chaplin's staggering success. The small tramp became a world-wide phenomenon in just two years. The character of a small tramp made Chaplin a wealthy man. A few years later, he established his own movie company along with other movie actors, earning a fortune and being the scriptwriter, actor, musician, producer and a distributor of his movies – all in one person.

In order to understand why people loved his character so much, we need to look at the situation in a wider context. Back then, when Chaplin became famous, the world was in chaos. World War I was

"WE THINK
TOO MUCH
AND FEEL
TOO LITTLE."
–
*Charles Spencer
Chaplin*

about to break out. The world was restless and full of evil. In these difficult times, the movie screen suddenly featured a sweet little guy with a top hat, moustache and a bamboo walking stick, walking in a funny way. That funny tramp was a character of odd and childish spirit, much resembling the real person – Charles Spencer Chaplin. Both characters had a controversial and complicated nature.

As Chaplin himself described his character: "A tramp, a gentleman, a poet, a dreamer, a lonely fellow, always hopeful of romance and adventure." The small tramp had no annoying responsibilities. He merrily wandered around and tried coping with life in his bizarre way. That kind of character injected hope in people in hard times. The spectators felt that the tramp represented something they secretly desired to resemble themselves.

Chaplin's dreams came true because instead of only fulfilling the tedious orders of a movie studio director, he was completely committed to his work and childishly noticed his chance to achieve something remarkable. This way, the homeless tramp Chaplin turned into a world-famous multi-millionaire and movie star.

GROWN-UPS ARE DECEITFUL, CHILDREN ARE HONEST

At first glance, it seems that children lie more than adults. Yes, children tend to fib or malarkey due to their ignorance or lack of experience. Grown-ups, on the other hand, lie about important things, and not only to others, but themselves as well.

Grown-ups don't dare to open themselves to their close ones and honestly say what they really expect from the relationship. But dishonesty in a relationship leads to its breaking. How can you love someone if you don't tell them what you think? A truly high-quality relationship between two people must be founded on honesty alone. Saying that, I don't mean the situation where some insignificant facts have not been discussed. There can be small secrets in a family. What I mean is honesty in fundamental issues, for example, in what partners expect from each other and what they can offer.

By the way, a general and simple rule applies in love to how to pick a partner for life. Following that rule can nip any kind of future deceit in the bud. You should pick a man or a woman that doesn't think you are ordinary, but special. This simple rule is one of the certain principles or love. Don't stop looking before you have

found someone that considers you special and who you consider special, because then you won't have to check what you say, but can be childishly honest all the time. If someone constantly sees faults in you, it means that they don't value your strengths enough – there's no point to waste your life on being with that person.

If a child wants something, they make it known explicitly and clearly. If a grown-up wants something, then instead of letting their wish be known in a straight way, they may start telling fables. People beat around the bush, make cryptic insinuations, try to manipulate and misguide others. But why do grown-ups lie in the first place? The answer is simple – people would rather follow their minds not their hearts. They let their mind misguide them.

Children follow their hearts. They can't construct long and intricate plans about how to influence someone's behavior. Children are sincere and open and just say what they want. They never leave it at that, when they think they are being hurt, or fail to sulk, when they don't get what they want. If you are childishly sincere and honest, others understand your intention and you will attract others with a similar world view. When you stop lying, you can start living happily and simply, because then you won't have to worry about what you have told someone anymore.

Examples about deceitfulness can be found in anything grown-ups do. Take the business world, for instance. Many people establish companies hoping to win customers over and become rich. They create a pretty image of how their product or service is essential to the masses. After some time, however, most business plans fail. Why? Because people running the business were actually dishonest to themselves and their customers. They didn't really offer products or services that were necessary enough to the customers.

At the same time, businessmen whose companies turn out to be success stories have been much more honest to their customers. They have focused on offering real value to their customers. And believe me, if a customer really gets the same thing for a lower price, or a better thing for the same price than somewhere else, they will buy it from

you. If customers sense the real savings and value they are offered, the company will be successful. But it all starts with complete honesty.

It's another story with intentionally wicked companies that have been created to trick people from the beginning. For example, they may use legal tricks, exploiting a legal loophole, or they may try tricking the customers with a manipulative sales strategy where customers are lied to. The loophole fixed sooner or later, and customers won't make repeat purchases when they've been deceived once. Also, they won't recommend that company to their friends. Those making shady transactions may temporarily trick out some money from customers, but these kinds of companies don't survive for long. Real value in business is still only created by being childishly honest to oneself and the customers.

I'll give you another example of deceitfulness. Grown-ups tend to judge those that have gone further than them. That's why rich people are gossiped about. The ones telling the stories are always the ones that aren't successful in their profession. In most cases, the stories are not true, as successful people mostly have an honest attitude. If the talkers would achieve anything themselves, they would immediately change their opinion. Therefore, I recommend that whatever you do, be childishly honest to both yourself and others. Be patient and don't try to earn a lot with just one or two transactions. Everything takes time. Easy come, easy go. An old saying goes that the one that wants a lot at once won't get anything slow and steady. You need to give the world as much you hope to get in return.

Grown-ups are deceitful, since their behavior is guided by the mind. Children are sincere and honest, and their behavior is guided by the heart. If you wish to advance in life and be happy, you must be childishly honest to yourself and others.

A STORY ABOUT CHILDISH HONESTY

Abraham Lincoln

Abraham Lincoln's nickname was Honest Abe. According to a legend, he earned that name around the age of 22 in Illinois, working as a shop assistant at a village shop in New Salem. Lincoln was a bit shy and clumsy back then, but always punctual and precise. He didn't want to take advantage of the customers' ignorance and always tried to redeem any mistakes that occurred.

One day, he sold goods to Mrs. Duncan that lived two miles away for 2 dollars and six cents. In the evening, when he was counting the till before closing up, Lincoln discovered that Duncan had paid six cents more than she had to. "This error must be corrected tonight," he told himself, and as soon as he closed the shop, he set out to take the till surplus back to the customer. The lady was just about to go to sleep when she heard a knock on the door.

Mrs. Duncan was very surprised when she saw the village shop assistant standing in the door. Lincoln apologized for the error, returned the six cents to the lady, and slept peacefully that night because he had rectified his error.

"NO MAN HAS A GOOD ENOUGH MEMORY TO BE A SUCCESSFUL LIAR."
–
Abraham Lincoln

On another occasion, a lady came in to the shop late in the evening when Lincoln was about to lock up. She bought a half pound of tea, weighed in a hurry. Right after the customer had left, Lincoln locked the shop and went home. On returning the next morning, his attention was called to the scales which had a four-ounce weight, instead of eight in them. He knew at once that he must have given the woman a quarter instead of a half pound of tea. Having weighed another quarter a pound, he closed the shop and took the missing half a pound of tea to the customer's home, apologizing for last night's mistake.

There are several similar stories about Lincoln's childish honesty. It's hard to say how truthful they are, but Lincoln is unquestionably deemed one of the greatest heroes and examples in US history for having managed to preserve America's integrity as a president during the Civil War and putting an end to slavery. A great part in that was played by his childish honesty. The people and confidants trusted him because he talked straight from his heart and his actions were childishly honest. Lincoln had a childish nature.

Socrates has said: "An honest man is always a child."

GROWN-UPS AVOID RISKS, CHILDREN LOOK FOR EXCITEMENT

Children are motivated by new opportunities – everything that promises excitement. Children adore it. Every new game and endeavor is like an adventure to the unknown, not knowing the result. Grown-ups give up excitement, because they are rather motivated by safety and maintaining it. Avoiding risk at all costs, grown-ups replace adventure and thrills for a safe and known result.

In some respects, it could be said that a person is a real grown-up from the moment he or she stops taking risks. Not taking risks, however, means deterioration. We would never have learnt how to sit up, hadn't we taken the risk that we might fall backwards and hit our head. Also, we would never have learnt how to walk, if we had constantly concentrated on getting hurt if we lost balance.

Children have no risk-oriented mind frame, while adults do. And this is good. It's bad when we map the risks and still decide not to act. If we as adults would see risk in a childish way, we would map the specific risk and hedge it as soon as possible, but act regardless of the risk.

There is a saying that any kind of action involves risk-taking, but it's many times smaller than the risk arising from inactivity. I completely agree with that idea. The biggest risk is inactivity. It's as good as giving up life and starting to wait for it to end. Loss is certain. This kind of life and degeneration is pointless, because we can't be happy or live like that.

If you have a childish attitude towards risk, you welcome difficulties the same way as you do victories. Even more, you should be grateful about the difficulties in your path. All nice and happy grown-ups have suffered misfortune and loss in their lives. These experiences put together have made them the shining and pleasant personalities that they are.

If you try to avoid disappointments and difficulties at all costs, you are living in a cocoon. Decide to live in a childishly dangerous way, not in an adult-like safe way. Grown-ups avoid danger, children look for thrills. Next time you are desperately afraid of doing something you know you should do inside, pose yourself the following question: "What is the worst that could happen to me if I do that?"

In most cases, you must accept that nothing bad will really happen to you – you probably won't get hurt or injured. Physically, nothing will probably happen to you, because the modern adult challenges are mostly of the mental variety.

The worst thing that could happen to you is someone else's scornful assessment about your failure or your own negative emotion – in any case, something insignificant. But now, ask another question: "What is the most extraordinary thing that could happen to me if I accept the challenge?"

Imagine how you defeat that challenge, and what kind of emotion you will get from that feeling of success. But if you really accomplish it, the emotion will be many times more powerful! The one that has acted despite of risks, and experiences success, will go through it again and again in the future. He or she will become a serial accomplisher.

If you act in a childish way, despite of risks, you will make your dreams come true and are happy. You will feel alive and enjoy your exciting and dangerous life.

If you refuse taking risks as an adult, you also refuse life itself and endless opportunities that life has in store for you. Start living in a childish way and looking for excitement, because then you can make your dreams come true and enjoy success and be happy.

A STORY ABOUT CHILDISHLY LOOKING FOR EXCITEMENT

—

Voltaire

Francois-Marie Arouet had 178 different pseudonyms during his life, Voltaire being the most famous one. Today, Voltaire is known as one of the greatest thinkers and writers of the Enlightenment. But if the following bizarre story that tells how Voltaire who had been born into an ordinary French middle-class family, managed to become outrageously rich, had never happened, we would probably have heard nothing about him. Because namely Voltaire's striking wealth gave his brilliant mind the unique opportunity to write about anything he wanted. He didn't have to worry about surviving, the public opinion, or anger of the elites because his writings were in sharp contradiction with the truth accepted by the public at the time.

The turning point in Voltaire's life came when he returned from exile in England and took part in a dinner organized by Charles du Fay. At that dinner, he met Charles Marie de la Condamine, an ingenious mathematician. Voltaire was experiencing financial difficulties back then, but Condamine introduced an idea to Voltaire of how to make a nice fortune – in a questionable way, but not by breaking the law.

"GOD GAVE US THE GIFT OF LIFE; IT IS UP TO US TO GIVE OURSELVES THE GIFT OF LIVING WELL."

–

François-Marie Arouet

Condamine himself was quite a wealthy man by that time, but he looked to increase his wealth even more. Since his plan foresaw outwitting the French government, he didn't want to risk his reputation and fortune. That is why he needed Voltaire. Although Voltaire was not rich or very famous back then, he was supremely charismatic, well connected and anti-government, which made him an ideal partner.

In the beginning of the XVIII century, the French government had issued a lot of government bonds. When there was economic recession in the 1720s, they were forced to lower the interest rates, which in turn significantly lowered the market price of the bonds. In this situation, the government struggled to sell new bonds. One of Minister of Finance Le Pelletier-Desforts' deputies had, however, a "brilliant" plan for improving bond sales.

His idea was as follows: give the bond owners an opportunity to buy a ticket to a lottery organized by the government, with the ticket price tied to the bonds. Bond owners had to pay 1/1000 of the value of their bond portfolio for a ticket. If they won, the bond owner would earn the nominal value of the bonds, which is much higher than the market price, plus 500,000 livres more on top. It was a sum that would have made the winner a rich man for a lifetime.

Unfortunately, the government's plan was incredibly flawed. In essence, people owning 1,000 livres in bonds had to pay 1 livre for a lottery ticket. Those holding 100,000 livres in bonds had to pay 100 livres for one lottery ticket. But the chances of winning were equal for both.

Condamine planned to buy bonds in bulk for cheap and divide them in packs of thousand. According to his calculations, the wins would exceed the invested money several times. So, Voltaire established a syndicate for buying bonds that were later exchanged for lottery tickets, just as Condamine had suggested.

The plan worked and the men received winnings in the sum of 500,000 livres every month. But while ordinarily, people wrote phrases like "good luck" or something similar on the back of lottery tickets, Voltaire often wrote mocking sentences about the government and the officials, as was customary to him, and then signed the bonds with made-up names. The government soon realized that most of the winnings go to a select few, and the syndicate with Voltaire as its head was brought to court.

Since they hadn't really done anything illegal, they could keep the winnings. In any case, the lottery was terminated immediately the case against Voltaire's syndicate had collapsed. In the end, Voltaire earned 500,000 livres for a bit more than a year's work, and the rest of the money was divided between the other members of the syndicate. Both Voltaire and de la Condamine were wealthy men after that.

Condamine continued his research. Among other things, he undertook the first scientific expedition to the Amazonas region, during which the Amazon basin was mapped for the first time. He also studied the question whether the Earth had a perfect shape or not (it turned out it didn't), and helped to define the meter.

Voltaire invested his money in next businesses, using inside information to increase his wealth, for it wasn't illegal in the 18th century France. That enabled him to become ridiculously rich, and he became an important Enlightenment person much due to his wealth. Voltaire lived the life of his dreams, childishly seeking excitement, and it paid off abundantly. Avoiding risks in an adult way and continuing to go on as a poor man, he would never have had the chance to present his valuable ideas to the wider public.

GROWN-UPS DON'T FOOL AROUND, CHILDREN FOOL AROUND

Grown-ups enjoy activities with a specific goal and a tangible result. Grown-up activities are reasonable and smart. Fooling around is not one of such activities, because it lacks clear objective and outcome. The only apparent objective of fooling around is maybe creating a joyful state of mind.

Children love fooling around. They like to play all kinds of tricks and silly pranks. Fooling around makes children lively and cheerful, and develops their creativity. Grown-ups despise fooling around, just like other childish and natural activities, and actually without a cause. Fooling around opens our senses, makes us joyful, and helps us to be more creative.

The business world is generally very adult-like and conservative. Fooling around hasn't had a place there for centuries. But in recent times, creative training courses have been organized to business managers, broadening their creativity with various techniques that all involve fooling around and loosening up. The business world has started to see a competition advantage in fooling around. For example, brainstorming is organized in the most valuable companies

in the world with an aim to offer totally random ideas, feel free and foolish.

The leading IT companies of the world, such as Google, Apple, Microsoft, Facebook and others, pay enormous attention to the work environment so that it would stimulate the workers' creativity and fooling around. Employees can spend time in special rest rooms and play rooms during business hours. The leaders of the business world have understood that fooling around is useful.

If fooling around is useful in the extremely adult-like and result-oriented business world, then it must be useful also in your life, whatever you do for a living. Start fooling around like a child, because this way, you unleash true creativity in yourself and find so ingenious solutions to difficult problems that you could only dream of with an adult attitude.

If you are such a grown-up that there is no place for fooling around in your day, your life will pass in a sad and sorrowful way. Fooling around is available to content grown-ups only, however. You

need to get along well with yourself and respect yourself enough. Because if you fool around, it means that you dare to demonstrate your stupidity and open yourself from an impractical, childish and at the same time cool side.

Grown-ups don't let go, they think in sync with rules. There are many rules and if you follow all of them, you can never do anything cool. But if we let go everything that is unreasonable, and only try to do reasonable things in our life, we give up on life itself. Joy and cheerfulness comes from borderline situations that are actually not reasonable or permissible.

Think about situations that have brought the most emotions and joy to your life. Did you behave in a restrained way, or was your rationality filter turned off in those moments? I believe that you discovered that all great moments of joy have been the times when we gave up being restrained and have had fun like children, doing something forbidden and unreasonable. Figuratively speaking, you can't jump in a puddle without making your clothes wet. If your clothes are wet, they can also become dirty and we can fall ill. From the rational perspective, having fun in puddles is unreasonable. But children need it because it makes them happy.

You can't always be reasonable. Grown-ups also need to "jump in a puddle" from time to time. We need activities that make us dirty but bring the more joy and emotions the more we do it. For a grown-up, puddle jumping may be changing a job, contacting an attractive person, or even buying an item of clothing, a car, or another commodity that we love, but may not be the most reasonable choice when thinking rationally.

An adult who doesn't have enough self-confidence or self-respect cannot afford fooling around. This remains true even if they are on their own, as they fear seeming less valuable in their own eyes. All children fool around, because they don't need to worry about what others think, as do all self-confident adults, because they also don't worry about other people's opinion.

If you don't trust yourself enough, you are cramped up and constantly observe your behavior. You don't want to be a laughing stock. Constantly observing yourself, it's impossible to fool around and feel totally free. In order to be completely free, you need to start fooling around in a childish way. If you don't dare to in the beginning, start with small pranks and move on from that, until you have become a totally brave and childishly playful prankster. Then, you will start enjoying life in a real way, and you are more productive in what you do.

Besides children, only those grown-ups dare to fool around, who are confident enough. Fooling around takes some courage and trusting oneself. If you start fooling around in a childish way, you will be more creative in your work, and will enjoy your activities more.

A STORY ABOUT CHILDISHLY FOOLING AROUND
—
Michael Schumacher

The description of the following events may seem like a good joke, but it is actually a real-life story about how Michael Schumacher took a cab to the airport.

Schumacher, the seven-time Formula 1 champion living in Switzerland, tool a plane to Germany in early December of 2007 to bring back a puppy from there. They landed near Coburg and drove 20 miles to Gehuelz by car, to pick up the new pet for the family. When Schumacher ordered a taxi to drive back to the airport, he noticed that they had quite little time for catching the plane.

Schumacher politely asked the taxi driver Tuncer Yilmaz to let him drive the cab himself during the 20 mile ride back to the airport. It's probably no surprise that the taxi driver complied with the odd request of the legendary racing driver, maybe also hoping to develop professionally. With his wife Corinna, their two children and the new family member Ed, an Australian shepherd pup, Schumi stepped on it and they were underway. Mr Tuncer Yilmaz watched in awe as the 38-year-old legend showed him how he should do his job.

As everybody knows, there are no speed limits on German highways. Yilmaz told the German newspaper Muenchner Abendzeitung: „I found myself in the passenger seat, which was strange enough, but to have Schumi behind the wheel of my cab was incredible." Although the vehicle was an Opel Vivaro minivan with a maximum speed of 100 miles per hour, Schumacher managed to squeeze everything out of it: "He drove at full throttle around the corners and overtook in some unbelievable places."

At the end of the ride, Schumi paid the 60 euro taxi fare and gave a handsome 100-euro tip to the taxi driver. When the seven-time Formula 1 world champion sits behind the wheel of a minivan to race to the airport at full speed, it can only be called a childish prank. This untraditional and cheerful attitude has made him one of the best F1 pilots of all time.

"I FEEL LIKE A KID WITH A NEW TOY ... A CHILD BEFORE CHRISTMAS."

–

Michael Schumacher

GROWN-UPS LOOK FOR PERFECTION, CHILDREN SETTLE FOR GOOD ENOUGH

Grown-ups feel constant stress and pressure over results. They look for perfection. We want to be faultless in our work, ideal partners, best friends, perfect parents, outstanding in our hobbies. We strive towards perfection in everything. But although our goals are high, nobody is really a faultless parent or partner. It's impossible to be perfect in everything.

Children don't look for perfection, they settle for good enough. Children don't expect the best food in the world for breakfast, but are satisfied with simple cornflakes. Children don't try to be best friends to their playmates, but they are exactly as good as they can be at the moment. Children don't feel the pressure to be perfect, and therefore never have trouble with what they do. Children don't feel stress in what they do like grown-ups do.

If you really want to achieve something and be happy, stop looking for perfection in everything. In the best case scenario, you can only be really good in one or two things. Nobody in the world is the best professionally while being an ideal parent and partner, not to mention being the best cook for their family or something similar. It's humanly impossible to achieve.

The media creates heroes. In the media, we meet ideal people that are the best in everything. But the media is biased because some aspect has to be intensified or some facts need to be shown in a better light to add value to the news. Poor unhappy adults who meet these ideal idols via media and feel guilty for not being perfect themselves.

Children know how to be satisfied with what they have and how. Happy grown-ups know it too. Happy and satisfying life is based on a person being childishly satisfied with what they've got, but trying to move on in a steady pace at the same time.

If you feel negative emotions, thinking about what you don't have or how far you are from perfection, you can never be happy. Better start trying in a childish way to be the best as you can. Life is absolutely imperfect. Enjoy that imperfection. Enjoy that your phone doesn't work properly, or that your new car is scratched, or that your spouse isn't perfect either. If your spouse would be perfect, he or she would be impossible to love. There's no need to strive for perfection in everything. Excessive perfectionism stirs up anger, anguish and powerlessness in us. If you start acting without hoping for perfection, you are relieved of a burden, and things will start moving along.

Many adults try to copy a social template. They strive towards an ideal based on public opinion. But children don't know anything about what might be ideal in other people's opinion. They just try to cope with life and do it the best they can, being themselves as much as they can. Grown-ups have too high expectations for life. These expectations don't allow them to enjoy life and feel joyful.

Grown-ups should strive for perfection within their own limits. Happy and satisfying life means that we become more and more perfect in being ourselves during our lives. It doesn't mean that we are perfect and ideal according to some average norm. Quite the contrary – becoming ourselves we become more liked by ourselves and our close ones that love and appreciate us for what we are. So, we are less ideal by someone else's norm, but it's inevitable. Only by looking for good enough in this childish way, can you be the real you and live happily!

Grown-ups strive towards some set ideal, while children just try to be as good as they can be, as themselves. Happy and satisfying life means that you try to become more perfect in being yourself throughout your life. It doesn't mean that you are perfect according by other people's standards, quite the contrary.

A STORY OF BEING CHILDISHLY SATISFIED
—
Robert De Niro

The 17-year-old Robert De Niro once came out from a movie theatre with a friend and suddenly declared that he was going to become a movie actor. No-one believed him. But then he dropped out from the senior year of high school and joined Stella Adler's acting school.

About ten years later, in the mid-1970s, Paul Schrader's manuscript, *Taxi Driver*, reached the table of the young movie director Martin Scorsese. The movie talks about a mentally unstable and schizophrenic Vietnam veteran that works night shifts as a taxi driver in New York. When the main character Travis decides to save the teenage prostitute Iris, the movie takes a very bloody turn.

Scorsese offered the role of Travis to Dustin Hoffman. Hoffman has said that he didn't accept the role because he thought Scorsese was crazy. He has regretted his decision later. When Scorsese offered the role to Robert De Niro, the young actor immediately liked the manuscript. They signed a 35,000 dollar contract and started working.

Before they had even started filming, De Niro won an Oscar for his previous role in *Godfather II*, so his value as an actor went up.

"TIME GOES ON.
SO WHATEVER
YOU'RE GOING
TO DO, DO IT. DO
IT NOW. DON'T
WAIT."
–
*Robert Anthony
De Niro Jr.*

The producers of Columbia Studios were now afraid that De Niro would ask for a deserved pay rise and started looking for excuses for stopping the production of the movie. But De Niro was childishly happy with the relatively tiny salary and told the movie producers that he would respect their initial agreement. It meant that they could still start filming the movie.

De Niro was thorough in preparing for the role – he worked as a taxi driver in 12-hour shifts, and he also learnt about mental illnesses. The hard work paid off, the movie earned numerous awards, and made De Niro famous as a valued actor.

He wasn't looking for ideal conditions, but just did his work well, investing all of his soul in it. Since that movie, De Niro hadn't had a reason to complain about lack of job offers or too small a salary. Only recently, in 2010, the movie, *Little Fockers*, came out, called complete junk by movie experts. The movie didn't win any prizes unlike *Taxi Driver*, except for the worst supporting actor award and other mock awards.

However, Robert De Niro cashed in a staggering 20 million dollars for playing in the movie! It was all because as an aspiring actor, he hadn't looked for the perfect conditions but childishly accepted the small income that was available.

CROWN-UPS COMPETE, CHILDREN DO THEIR OWN THING

Grown-ups' attention is focused on competing with others, constantly trying to be better than the Joneses. Women compare whether they are fitter than their girlfriend; men compare whether they have a better job, more money or a prettier wife than their friend. At work, grown-ups make careers by pushing a colleague aside to get past.

Children's attention is focused on doing their own thing. They go quietly about their games and don't try to be better than their playmates in everything. Grown-ups' wish to beat others in things is connected with negativity, because trying to win at any cost, we actually hope others do badly. In this competition, there are no winners, because those that are better, actually lose, as although their performance was better, wishing bad things for a competitor creates so many negative emotions in them that they can't enjoy their victory.

Positive and productive competition means trying to give our best and not caring about being better than others whatever it takes. All our attention is focused on improving our performance, not competing with others. If we do our thing like children and cooperate with others, we will achieve the best possible result.

If life was a car race, many grown-ups would try to win by ramming the main contenders off the track. But that kind of winning tastes bitter. Although we have won, we didn't actually improve, we just pushed our rivals off the track. We weren't faster, our competitors were just slower. When we get on the track next time, we will be tackled and pushed off the track, and then we will be among those that didn't complete the race.

In case of progressive competition or by doing our own thing like a child, we drive as fast as we can and try to win by honest means. Honest competition motivates us to try and practice harder. By this kind of competitive but brotherly synergy rivals help each other, becoming better together.

To be happy, I advise you not to concentrate on victory but the beauty of the game. If you set the beauty of the game as your goal,

you will enjoy the race and victory is just an extra bonus, not an aim in itself. If your goal is to beat someone in an adult manner, you will always be miserable in both winning and losing.

In major corporations, it's typical that while making a career, people don't focus on their work but use dishonest methods to achieve a faster result. They slander their competitors and throw sand in the gears of their colleagues. Relationships, behind-the-scenes plotting and politics are what matters. This adult work environment is negative. Truly successful companies motivate their workers to engage in childishly positive and competitive cooperation instead of focusing on beating each other.

All big success stories are based on the wish to accomplish something noble, necessary and good, without trying to be better than someone else at all costs, but create something novel. You can become really successful and happy by childishly enjoying the beauty of the game, not by trying to be better than others at all costs. Instead of beating others, focus on doing your own thing – there are always better chances in that!

Grown-ups are focused on being better than others, while children do their thing as well as they can, enjoying the process while they do it. If you compete with dishonest methods, whishing your competitors to do badly, you have lost anyway, even if you finish first. Real success comes from childishly competing together and wishing your competitors well.

A STORY ABOUT CHILDISHLY DOING YOUR OWN THING

—

Christopher Columbus

Columbus started his sea travels at the age of 15 and dedicated his life to sailing from there on. When Columbus had sailed all kinds of seas and taken part in expeditions for two decades, he was convinced that when sailing west from Europe, it was possible to discover a shorter trade route to India.

Now, he needed money to realize his brave idea. Thus, he first went to talk to the king of Portugal. The king listened to Columbus' proposal and submitted it to a committee. The committee refused the application due to its high cost.

The king's advisors believed that Columbus got the distance calculations wrong and that in reality, the trip would be much longer. (They were right, as it later turned out.) This venture would have also contradicted Portugal's plans regarding the existing trade route around Africa. After the refusal by Portuguese authorities, he took his son and moved to Spain to present his idea to the rulers there, namely King Ferdinand and Queen Isabella.

The Spanish monarchs were too preoccupied with fighting the Moors to listen to the proposal. After two years of lobbying, he got

"YOU CAN NEVER CROSS THE OCEAN UNTIL YOU HAVE THE COURAGE TO LOSE SIGHT OF THE SHORE."

–

Cristoforo Colombo

a chance to present his idea to the committee. His application was again refused. The reason was similar as in case of Portugal.

If Columbus had worried about his reputation, he would have given up. Most European rulers found Columbus to be mad, and ignored him. But he didn't pay attention to the rulers' opinion and continued to make his idea a reality.

While Columbus escorted Spanish monarchs during their wartime travels, he sent his brother to present his idea to the monarchs of England and France. His brother's attempts were unsuccessful, and it seemed that Christopher Columbus would suffer the same fate. In late 1491, Columbus presented his idea to the rulers of Spain for the final time, and he was refused again, this time because of his greater demands.

Columbus had just given up and about to go to France when he was notified that Luis de Santangel, the king's treasurer, had managed to convince king Ferdinand to change his mind a couple of weeks after the negotiations. The Spanish monarchs were now happy to finance his voyage.

Columbus had, by that time, held futile negotiations with different monarchs for eight years. We don't know what would have become of America and world history if Columbus had had an adult-like and competitive attitude towards the whole venture and if he had worried about other people's opinion.

He was considered mad, but he didn't give up childishly doing his own thing. And although the experts were right and he didn't find a trade route to India, his childish action led him to something bigger instead – the discovery of a new continent, America.

GROWN-UPS ARE HYPOCRITICAL, CHILDREN ARE SINCERE

A person's attitude is characterized well by their attitude towards their subordinates. Grown-ups tend to think that people should treat their bosses better than their subordinates because it might prove beneficial in the future. Children take all people equally. They can't make rational choices like that. Adults should act in a similar way because favoring superiors instead of subordinates is prime example of hypocrisy. It won't be beneficial to that person in the long run. People around us sense the insincerity and selfish sucking up of the hypocritical person.

The more adult-like the person, the harder it is to understand if their opinion or answer is honest and if their words are sincere. Adults tend to say what they think their companion wants to hear, not what they would really like to hear. They also ask questions out of politeness, although they are not in the least bit interested in hearing the answer. This kind of behavior is definitely insulting to the sincere responder.

If you want to start living in a way that the surrounding people respect and love you, you must at first be sincere. Be honest to yourself and others. How can you be happy, if you don't dare to be yourself? How could you be successful, if you keep worrying about what other people think? This kind of constraining yourself is frustrating and it wastes your energy.

Try to be as honest like a child. Say what you think. You don't have to be brutally rude. Start by expressing your opinion honestly, without fearing what others may think of it. For some time, the adult insincerity may be useful, but in the long term, no one respects a person that doesn't have a personal opinion and who only says what others want to hear.

Think about a charismatic person for a moment that you look up to. Think about someone that you would enjoy spending time with and that could be set as an example to others. Now, try to imagine how charming or interesting that person would be if he or she didn't say what they think: if they were hypocritical and manipulative in an adult manner. You probably would conclude that

the person has earned other people's respect partly thanks to his or her sincerely and nature to say what they think. It's impossible to be happy, holding back all the time. You must feel free like a child does, because only then is it possible for you to be happy.

Children are sincere; grown-ups tend to say what they think their companion wants to hear. In order to be happy, you must become more childish and sincere. Only then can you create high-quality close relationships and earn other people's respect.

A STORY ABOUT CHILDISH SINCERITY
—
Muhammad Ali

Do you know who the current heavyweight boxing-champion is? I don't. During the heyday of Muhammad Ali, even those that were totally ignorant in sports knew who the current champion was. In 1966, Ali received call to the army – the Vietnam War was underway. Muhammad refused army service, justifying it with his religious convictions. He had recently accepted Islam. Ali announced that he wasn't going to serve in Vietnam and said: "I ain't got no quarrel with them Viet Cong," and added, "No Vietcong ever called me nigger."

By then, Ali had been unbeatable in all of his 29 professional matches and knew very well that he was risking with punishments that could hinder his career, such as depravation of liberty or removal from a sports event. Harald Conrad, Ali's promoter, told the Times magazine: "Overnight he became a 'nigger' again. He threw his life away on one toss of the dice for something he believed in. Not many folks do that."

Ali was punished with five years of imprisonment, a 10,000 dollar fine, deprivation of his champion title, and disqualification from

future competitions. Ali appealed the decision and in 1971, the case reached the Supreme Court. It was decided there that he had the right to be excused from the army because his beliefs are based on religious teachings that are against any kind of warfare and that his protest had been sincere.

After staying away for three and a half years, he could return in the boxing ring and continue his career. Muhammad Ali behaved in total sincerity and childishness, when he remained true to himself and refused to do something that was against his conscience. At first, it seemed that it was a brave but wrong decision, because he lost four years of his career as a sportsman. In hindsight, however, it may be said that thanks to his childish naiveté, he became a legend – Ali became one of the spokesmen against the Vietnam War.

The clock kept ticking and increasing numbers of American soldiers were killed in Vietnam. More and more people stood behind Muhammad Ali's anti-war point of view. Ali's childishness raised on the level of world leaders from the level of top boxers.

"I'M SO FAST THAT LAST NIGHT I TURNED OFF THE LIGHT SWITCH IN MY HOTEL ROOM AND WAS IN BED BEFORE THE ROOM WAS DARK."

–
Cassius Marcellus Clay, Jr.

GROWN-UPS COPY, CHILDREN CREATE

In this day and age, there is a great demand for people with professional qualifications and a creative capacity on top of that. Needless to say, creative people are just as valued outside their work for being joyful and interesting companions. In addition to professional success, creativity helps you to remain positive and happy, because a creative and inquisitive mind helps you to find solutions to even the most difficult problems.

In a creative mood, all your senses and your heart is engaged in a captivating activity that in turn makes you feel happy, excited and contented. Creativity is a rare gift among grown-ups. Grown-ups are masterful copycats, who always want to do things in a way someone else has done before them. They are afraid of making mistakes and thinking on their own. If someone has a creative idea, it's usually first criticized, saying that no one has ever done it like that. It seems that the only possible way of doing something is in a way it's always been done.

But if someone has created something successful, the copycats emerge. They use their whole mind, making all the effort they can,

but they still don't reach the level of the original thing that was copied. One can never achieve anything so remarkable by copying that they can achieve by being childishly creative.

Children don't know anything about how things have been done before. They just learn, develop, and try to do things in a way that seems right to them during their activity. Children act in a creative way. They find creative solutions for doing things better as they go.

If you as an adult can leave aside all your previous experience and knowledge, concentrating creatively on solving the problem, completely new ideas will spark up in your mind. All adults that have achieved something outstanding have absolutely always been creative personalities. Creative personalities aren't only the ones with a beret, sweater and a scarf, but everyone that uses creativity and finds novel solutions in their work.

In order to be creative, we must forget about the old. Our old experience doesn't go anywhere, because intuition automatically considers it while creating new solutions. But we mustn't get stuck

in the existing things. For example, we can't drive a car by only looking in the rear mirror. We need to check what's going on behind us from time to time, but in order to drive successfully, our main focus must be on what's going on ahead, because then we instinctively make the right decisions: where to turn, when to break and when to accelerate.

It's the same in real life. We can't live by looking at things that have already been done all the time. By copying, constantly fearing being wrong, you will never feel true joy of creating something new. In a similar way, you can never feel other people's admiration and approval. You will always remain secondary.

But if you start childishly playing with new ideas and opportunities, you will soon discover that you have created something new.

These moments offer excitement and enthusiasm that are work a risk. In order to achieve something creative, you must dare to risk with a possibility of utter failure. With a childish attitude, you will be able to bare such failures and start creating from scratch. With an adult attitude, you are so afraid of failure that you never dare to come up with new original solutions. Then, you will also never be totally happy and satisfied.

Grown-ups like to copy everything that has been done before. Children no nothing about what's been done before. They act creatively, finding new solutions as they go along. If you as an adult act in a childishly creative way, you will feel happy about having created something new, and you will also be recognized. Without applying creativity, you will never be able to be truly happy.

A STORY ABOUT CHILDLIKE CREATIVITY
—
Pablo Picasso

When talking about childlike creativity, Picasso may surely be considered the prime example. He was the most famous and influential artist of the 20th century, and one of the creators of a completely new art form called cubism.

Picasso's style was technically masterful, creative as expected from a visionary, and deeply empathic. He changed his style so drastically several times during his life that it seems as if it's five or six artists instead of one. By the way, his full name consists of 23 different words. This long full name pays respect to various relatives and saints.

However, in 1900, the artist started using only the family name Picasso from his mother's side as a signature.

In his childhood, Picasso was a serious and mature child. His jet black eyes had a piercing glance that as if predicted a great future for him. Picasso recounted: "When I was a child, my mother told me: "When you become a soldier, you'll become a general. If you become a monk, you'll end up as a pope." Instead, I became a painter, and I became Picasso."

Many aspiring artists would like to paint like Picasso. Specialists from different fields would like to be as creative in their work as Picasso was in his art.

How did that artist manage to be so creative and outstanding? What was his secret? How could he exclude any kind of rational copying?

Picasso has hinted in his talks that his life's credo has been never to grow up.

Picasso believed that if a person sought wisdom for a long enough time, he would reach a childish attitude once again: „It takes a very long time to become young".

He said that childish virtue is what grown-ups should try to find in themselves in order to achieve good results. „Every child is an artist. The problem is how to remain an artist once we grow up".

Picasso thought that grown-ups aren't free in their thoughts and action, they surrender to the pressure of the public and other influencing factors: „The older you get the stronger the wind gets – and it's always in your face".

The great artist believed that a person can have a childish attitude at any age: „Youth has no age".

He didn't believe in aging in the common sense of the word, but saw it as an opportunity to become even better: „We don't grow older, we grow riper".

Picasso knew that a person that wants to become a real artist needs to forget everything and start from an empty page, with a childlike attitude: „What might be taken for a precocious genius is the genius of childhood. When the child grows up, it disappears without a trace. It may happen that this boy will become a real painter someday, or even a great painter. But then he will have to begin everything again, from zero".

Picasso looked for opportunities throughout his life of painting in a more and more childish way:

„It took me four years to paint like Raphael, but a lifetime to paint like a child."

Yes, Pablo Picasso was a creator with a truly childish attitude.

"THE CHIEF ENEMY OF CREATIVITY IS GOOD SENSE."

–

Pablo Diego José Francisco de Paula Juan Nepomuceno María de los Remedios Cipriano de la Santísima Trinidad Martyr Patricio Clito Ruíz y Picasso

GROWN-UPS DEVELOP THEIR WEAKNESSES, CHILDREN DEVELOP THEIR STRENGTHS

Grown-ups like to be at a relatively good level in everything they do. We try to polish our weaknesses to achieve an average level at everything. We are afraid to be left behind and stick out with our incompetence.

The glorification of mediocrity begins in school. In school, they teach all children, everyone a personality and with their special gifts, by the same standards. Everyone must be average in everything. Children are demanded to have equal abilities in all subjects.

I remember an old cartoon that characterized the nature of school. It was a school for animals. From one door, all kinds of different animals came in – bears, rabbits, foxes, wolves – and on the other side, there was a conveyor line with exactly the same kind of chickens sitting in a row. Life does the same to us all the time – polishes our sharpness into bluntness.

Everywhere, mediocrity is favored and individuality is put down. Being special or unique rather seems to be the privilege of actors, singers, top athletes and other superstars. Children don't develop their weaknesses, because they're not interested in that. Children want to do interesting and exciting things. It doesn't probably surprise you, but what attracts them is usually what they're good at as well.

The heart knows exactly for what we have the prerequisites to be the best at, and our interest always shows, where our real talents lie. Grown-ups, however, struggle all they can to polish their weak spots, blend in the mass and get satisfactory results in everything.

The fact is that every person is the odd one in some environment. It's not something to be fought against, because it's a completely normal situation. Imagine a lawyer in a suit appearing in the midst of hippies who are drinking beer on the beach. In that situation, the lawyer probably feels uncomfortable and inappropriate. The more outstanding and special a person is, the more bizarre he or she looks in a specific environment.

For example, geniuses don't often cope with regular life at all, because they are slightly autistic or have other social disorders. At the same time, they give so much to the society with their creation that we shouldn't expect them to blend in and be completely normal people. If you want to be completely happy with your life, I recommend you to develop only those sides that are strong – just as children do.

By polishing your weaknesses, you will only achieve an average level. But if the same energy is invested in your strengths, it's a much more enjoyable and interesting process and the result will be much more satisfying as well. This way, you will become a special person with your own talents.

In general, people aren't born masters but become one when they start investing in those characteristics that have the potential to develop into being extraordinary. People mistakenly think that those that achieve great results in some field are the chosen ones and don't even seem to try very hard. If someone works on their talents constantly, it doesn't have to look like hard work to a bystander. For someone that develops his or her talents, the whole process is interesting and satisfying, and everyone he or she goes, the talents develop as if on their own.

This is happiness – to do something that makes your heart beat with anticipation, and get better while doing it. If you childishly only do what you really like during your whole life, you will be more talented when you are older as well. This way, you can be the real you and enjoy life.

Grown-ups develop their weaknesses and strive towards mediocrity. Children follow their interests and therefore develop their talents. If you are engaged in your strengths, i.e. what you really like, then you will live a satisfying and happy life!

A STORY ABOUT CHILDISHLY DEVELOPING ONE'S STRENGTHS

—

Steven Spielberg

When you are watching a movie that you really love, it's likely that it might be directed by Steven Spielberg. Spielberg is probably the best-known and wealthiest Hollywood movie maker. He has made so many blockbusters that it's pointless to list them here. In addition to the hearts of viewers, he has also won the absolute support of movie critics.

When the small Steven was 6 years old, he saw his first movie. It was *The Greatest Show on Earth*. The movie presented circus, train accidents and clowns. The movie had a great impact on Steven. He spent most of his younger years trying to recreate his memories of these exciting scenes by crashing together toy trains and later filming this crash on a Kodak lens. He first got the taste of glory and honor at the age of 12 while being a boy scout, when he got a prize for his 9-minute western that he called *The Last Gunfight*.

Since that moment, Steven knew exactly what to do with his life. But everything doesn't always go according to plan.

When Steven's parents Leah and Arnold got divorced, he and his father went to the state of Arizona where he went to the Arcadia

"WHEN I GREW
UP, I STILL
WANTED
TO BECOME
A MOVIE
DIRECTOR."
–
*Steven Allan
Spielberg*

High School. In that period, Spielberg was an outcast among his peers and was persecuted as a Jewish child. The situation got even worse for Steven when he failed twice at the movie school entrance exams despite of his apparent talent. He then entered California State University study English as his father had desired.

Steven Spielberg remembers that his father wanted him to have a Plan B if his director's career was not going to be successful, "My father wanted me to be a teacher because it was a noble profession." Soon, Steven stopped fulfilling his father's dream and dropped out of college to make his own dream come true.

He had already started working at Universal Studios. He worked seven days a week for no pay at all! He was enthusiastically working on a short movie, *Amblin*. When the movie was finally completed, it changed Spielberg's life. He got the attention of studio managers and got a long-term contract offer. This was the beginning of his career. He later called his personal movie studio Amblin Entertainment.

Steven Spielberg didn't dream of becoming famous. He didn't dream about making money. He didn't even dream of winning Oscars. He just dreamed about making movies and developing his strengths in a childish way. That is why he gave up his college studies and started working as an unpaid intern at the movie studio.

The former unpaid intern is now one of the wealthiest people in the movie industry. If he had followed his father's back-up plan, there would be another mediocre English teacher in the world (because he didn't really like teaching). But we would be deprived of many great movies.

GROWN-UPS WAIT FOR CHANGES, CHILDREN MAKE CHANGES

Grown-ups hope that changes will be introduced in their lives from outside. Some wait for a lottery win, others an imminent promotion or that shops would lower their prices. It would be nice if the government raised pension premiums or child support. Instead of making things happen, it's always easier to find excuses and expect changes to come from the outside.

Grown-ups are like sleeping cats waiting for a mouse to run in their mouths. Since grown-ups are smart, they never fail at finding excuses. Some grown-ups say that they are too young for their dream to come true; others are afraid that it's too late and they are too old. Some believe that they are ill-educated; others that they are over-educated to fulfill their simple dream. There are millions of excuses – every time we are engulfed by fear, we can just hope for good luck and stop striving towards our dream to fulfill, finding an ideally suitable excuse.

Children's thoughts are very simple. They don't know how to hope that some external changes would do things for them. They just start fulfilling their dream gradually. They do everything in their power. Look at how a child moves towards a new and interesting toy. They don't expect an adult to turn up and give it to them. They don't wait, hoping for some external factors that are independent of their will.

Instead of finding endless excuses, simply do everything in your power, and things will start moving. If you start acting in a brave and childish manner, the external factors will work for you as well. Fortune favors the bold and enthusiastic! Stop feeling sorry for yourself and finding excuses. Your life isn't any more difficult than

any other's. Everyone has encountered misfortune and problems in their lives, but you should concentrate on these and present them as excuses.

Some adults make excuses that their parents were drunks or they had no parents at all. Some suffered from domestic violence or were teased at school. Whatever your excuse might be, let go of your past right now and simply do everything in your power.

Approximately 800 years ago, Saint Francis created this prayer: "God, grant me the serenity to accept the things I cannot change; the courage to change the things I can; and the wisdom to know the difference."

This prayer captures the idea of making things happen in a childlike manner. By finding excuses in an adult way, we are never able to fulfill our dreams. Everybody whose life is blessed with wonderful things has introduced these things in their lives themselves. At first, it may seem to us as if some positive changes have come to other people's lives from outside, but we simply don't know what they have done to introduce these changes. Start acting in a childish way right now and bring the changes in your life yourself!

Grown-ups wait for changes to come in the lives from outside. Children bring changes in their lives themselves. If you want to change your life and fulfill your dreams, start acting right away, like a child. Do everything in your power – then, the surrounding environment will help you. Fortune favors the brave and enthusiastic!

A STORY ABOUT CHILDISHLY
MAKING CHANGES

—

Coco Chanel

Coco Chanel was one of the most influential designers of her time. Every woman, even if she has never bought an original Chanel product, definitely has something that is inspired by the iconic designer.

The childhood of the famous fashion designer was everything but glamorous. She was born in 1883 in a correctional facility of Loire Valley where her single mother worked. After her mother's death, Coco's father, a travelling merchant, placed her daughter in the children's home. Coco Chanel was raised by nuns that taught her to sew. She spent her summers with her working-class relatives in Moulin where she developed her tailoring skills even further. That skill acquired by chance later led to her life's work.

Before going to the fashion industry, Chanel made short career as a club singer where she acquired the nickname Coco that she later adopted in fashion industry. Chanel started seaming hats and moved on to clothes. During her career, she made several revolutionary and childish changes that completely contradicted with the understanding of the time, but were at the same time so natural and necessary.

"IN ORDER TO BE IRREPLACEABLE ONE MUST ALWAYS BE DIFFERENT."
–
Gabrielle Bonheur Chanel

At the end of the 19th century, when Chanel was born, the high-class ladies of France wore corsets, puffy skirts and hats with feathers. The rebellious Chanel had a completely different vision. She said, "Luxury must be comfortable, otherwise it is not luxury."

Chanel was one of the first women to wear trousers in public. When she became famous and influential in the fashion world, many high society ladies started following her example. At the beginning of the 20th century, the high-society dresses were wide, boisterous and colorful. Coco found this abundant diversity to be tasteless and created an elegant black dress. When it was published in the Vogue fashion magazine in 1926, she named it Chanel Ford after the Ford Model T.

It was a revolution – the dress was simple and beautiful, and at the same time accessible to all women regardless of their social ranking. The dress won the hearts of the women of the post-war generation who found clothes restrained with corsets old-fashioned and impractical. It is nearly a century from the triumph of the little black dress, but it's still on the throne.

Once, Coco Chanel saw the blue and white striped fisherman's clothes and sailor uniforms on a trip to the French seaside. She found them beautiful and it inspired her so much that she created a clothes collection with sailor stripes. The striped clothes symbolized the practical outfits of the working class of the time, but Coco made them desirable for the high society.

On another occasion, Coco Chanel, then at the top of her fame, returned from a Mediterranean cruise where she had been exposed to too much sun. Since the times of Ancient Rome, pale complexion was in high esteem among the upper class because it indicated a noble life that enabled staying in during most of the free time. Dark skin, on the other hand, was connected with slavery, showing that people were moiling in the fields all day long. But since Chanel was a true fashion icon who was closely observed and followed, it became another fashion trend – sunbathing went into fashion.

Coco Chanel didn't expect for changes that were completely logical and necessary to just happen. Instead, she childishly made them happen herself and went down in history as a fashion icon. And who knows – if it hadn't been for Coco Chanel, maybe women would still be wearing corsets and avoiding trousers. The elegance of the little black dress would also be unknown to us, just like the striped sailor-style clothes. And we would fear the sunlight like fire.

Summary

The wisdom and experience grown-ups gather over their lives give them a rational attitude and don't allow them to enjoy their life to the fullest or make their dreams come true. The wisdom of adults works against them. It's easier for children to be happy because their way of thinking is simple.

In order to live childishly sincerely and have positive emotions as an adult, you must cast aside this wisdom and experience and adopt a childish approach to life. Don't worry, your wisdom won't disappear, quite the contrary – by adopting a childish attitude, you can apply your wisdom much more productively. You can't enjoy the sunrise if you start analyzing instead of sensing it. You can't become inspired if you already know everything.

All happy people, without exception, have a childlike attitude. Even their eyes shine as those of children. They follow their hearts and do what their soul desires. Having a rational attitude, you can't enjoy life or feel true enthusiasm and joy.

If you wish to fulfill your dreams, you must approach them as children – with enthusiasm and without doubts. When you start living your life with a childish attitude, you will start playing instead of working. Where grown-ups see difficulties, you will see opportunities. In a situation where people compete, you will peacefully do your thing. You don't look for perfection everywhere; you will be satisfied with what life has in store for you.

If you decide to live like a childlike grown-up, you will have adventures like Einstein, live in the moment like Rihanna, seek thrills like Voltaire, sulk like Michelangelo and enjoy life like Johnny Depp.

As a childish person, you won't surrender to your fears, you will happily greet difficulties and challenges. As a childish person, you can wonder about small things as well, and have fun instead of worrying.

If there is something you should remember from this book after ten or thirty years, it might be the title: "Never grow up". If you remember that phrase, it will help you to turn the adult attitude into a childlike one and be happy.

If you encounter a moment in your life where you can't make a decision and you don't know which path to follow, always choose the childish direction. Don't pick the easy road, but the more exciting and natural one. Your intuition will always give you the right answer. I wish you an exciting life and never growing up!

References

http://www.brainyquote.com

http://www.goodreads.com

http://www.nndb.com/people/670/000118316

http://www.biography.com/people/rihanna-201257#early-life

http://www.people.com/people/rihanna/biography

http://rihanna-fenty.com/biography-and-facts

http://courantblogs.com/sound-check/storrs-native-evan-rogers-discovered-rihanna-co-wrote-for-donny-osmond-n-sync

Rihanna (Megastars), Bridget Heos 2011

http://www.peoplewithimpact.com/rihanna/f44r89

http://www.patentdrafting.com/edison.htm

http://www.kazantoday.com/WeeklyArticles/oprah-winfrey.html

http://www.aceshowbiz.com/celebrity/oprah_winfrey/biography.html

http://www.thisdaylive.com/articles/why-ronaldo-dedicates-la-decima-glory-to-old-friend/179586

http://www.biography.com/people/cristiano-ronaldo-555730

http://www.elvis.com.au/presley/vernon_and_gladys_talked_about_raising_
   young_elvis_1956.shtml#sthash.bXFLQq3D.hryGdNq8.dpbs

http://www.snopes.com/music/artists/presley2.asp

http://www.biography.com/people/mark-twain-9512564?page=1

http://www.americaslibrary.gov/aa/twain/aa_twain_name_2.html

http://www.mensxp.com/entertainment/top-10s/12376-[birthday-special]-10-
   things-you-never-knew-about-john-lennon.html

http://exquisitelyboredinnacogdoches.blogspot.com/2009/01/john-len-
   non-liked-monopoly.html

http://www.beatlesinterviews.org/db1969.0503.beatles.html

http://www.nasa.gov/centers/glenn/about/bios/neilabio.html

http://www.wired.com/autopia/2012/08/neil-armstrong-aircraft

http://www.history.com/news/celebrating-the-75th-anniversary-of-snow-white-
   and-the-seven-dwarfs

http://www.mouseplanet.com/9365/Of_Failure_and_Success_The_Journey_
   of_Walt_Disney

http://whatthafact.com/interesting-facts-about-leonardo-da-vinci

http://www.leonardodavincisinventions.com/inventions-for-flight/leonar-
   do-da-vinci-landing-gear

http://www.theguardian.com/artanddesign/jonathanjonesblog/2011/nov/30/
   leonardo-da-vinci-animal-rights-activist

http://www.theredheadriter.com/2012/05/artist-leonardo-da-vinci-53-inter-
   esting-facts

http://www.biography.com/people/leonardo-da-vinci-40396#synopsis

http://news.moviefone.com/2013/05/10/18-things-you-didnt-know-about-leon-
   ardo-dicaprio

http://www.entrepreneur.com/article/197544

http://history1900s.about.com/od/people/a/gandhi_4.htm

http://www.uncoverdiscover.com/facts/10-things-you-did-not-know-about-ma-
   hatma-gandhi/gandhi-was-a-walking-enthusiast

http://www.history.com/topics/salt-march

http://science.howstuffworks.com/innovation/famous-inventors/what-did-al-
   bert-einstein-invent.htm

http://www.sailingscuttlebutt.com/2013/03/21/albert-einstein-not-much-of-a-sailor

http://content.time.com/time/magazine/article/0,9171,993017,00.html

http://einstein.biz/quotes.php

http://history.inrebus.com/index.php?category=15

http://www.biography.com/people/wolfgang-mo-zart-9417115#death-and-legacy&awesm=~oFEghOWzaaWviB

http://www.biography.com/people/sophia-loren-9386318?page=2

http://www.biography.com/people/cary-grant-9318103#films-of-1930s-and-1940s&awesm=~oFKljiBdrR46Fi

http://www.theguardian.com/politics/2013/apr/09/margaret-thatcher-falk-lands-gamble

http://en.mercopress.com/2013/04/08/falklands-war-a-turning-point-for-mar-garet-thatcher-s-image-and-political-fortunes

http://rt.com/news/falklands-division-thatcher-argentina-637

http://100swallows.wordpress.com/2008/05/10/michelangelo-and-the-cheap-skate-1

http://www.biography.com/people/michelangelo-9407628#liter-ary-works-and-personal-life&awesm=~oG7phdflZLQjyE

Carlin, John (2012). Rafa: My Story. New York: Hyperion Books.

http://www.2jesus.org/inspstories/analogy.html

http://www.jkrowling.com/en_GB/#/timeline/it-all-started

http://www.factmonster.com/spot/harrycreator1.html

http://abcnews.go.com/Entertainment/guinness-world-records-2012-photos/story?id=14521361

http://moviesdrop.com/2013/09/interesting-johnny-depp-facts-2142

https://uk.movies.yahoo.com/johnny-depp-nearly-fired-pirates-caribbe-an-161800362.html

http://www.yurtopic.com/society/history/henry-ford.html

http://www.fastcompany.com/3002809/be-henry-ford-apprentice-yourself-failure

http://www.biography.com/people/dalai-lama-9264833#awesm=~oClv-VtWQzEtHFS

http://www.myrkothum.com/the-10-very-best-zen-stories

http://www.biography.com/news/the-14th-dalai-lama-celebrates-his-77th-birth-day-20872417

http://www.itsnotmagicitsscience.com/science.asp?newsid=382

http://whatthafact.com/interesting-facts-about-mother-teresa

http://popularinfographics.com/mother-teresa

http://www.yurtopic.com/society/people/mother-teresa-facts.html

http://news.stanford.edu/news/2005/june15/jobs-061505.html

http://www.biography.com/people/steve-jobs-9354805

http://www.winstonchurchill.org/learn/biography/war-correspondent

http://www.biography.com/people/winston-churchill-9248164#early-life

http://mentalfloss.com/article/22037/magazine-sneak-peek-winston-church-ills-incredible-prison-break

http://www.express.co.uk/expressyourself/300007/Winston-Churchill-s-great-escape

http://thebestten.wordpress.com/2009/12/31/chapter-2-love-and-basketball

https://espn.go.com/sportscentury/features/00016048.html

http://www.naturalheightgrowth.com/2013/03/05/a-scientific-theory-on-why-playing-basketball-may-indeed-make-young-teenagers-increase-in-height-and-grow-taller

http://www.businessinsider.com/10-things-you-didnt-know-about-bill-gates-2011-4?op=1

https://www.goodreads.com/work/quotes/18353621-laughing-buddha-the-al-chemy-of-euphoric-living

http://voices.yahoo.com/interesting-facts-fat-laughing-buddha-8591861.html?cat=7

http://www.theguardian.com/film/filmblog/2014/jan/27/charlie-chaplin-tramp-birth-hero

http://www.history.com/this-day-in-history/first-appearance-of-little-tramp

http://www.biography.com/people/charlie-chaplin-9244327#early-career

http://www.notablebiographies.com/Ch-Co/Chaplin-Charlie.html

http://www.lookandlearn.com/blog/17590/charlie-chaplin-from-east-end-mu-sic-hall-to-hollywood

http://www.characterjournal.com/what-honesty-did-for-abraham-lincoln

http://www.biography.com/people/abraham-lincoln-9382540#awesm=~oFy-puYHkY3GIE9

http://www.todayifoundout.com/index.php/2013/05/how-voiltaire-made-a-fortune-rigging-the-lottery

http://www.biography.com/people/voltaire-9520178
http://www.damninteresting.com/the-enlightenment-guide-to-winning-the-lottery

http://www.telegraph.co.uk/news/worldnews/1572241/Michael-Schumacher-drives-taxi-in-airport-dash.html

http://www.imdb.com/name/nm1635856/bio

http://www.mirror.co.uk/tv/tv-news/70-facts-robert-de-niro-2171879

http://www.imdb.com/title/tt0075314/trivia

http://www.mrqe.com/lists/deniro/robert-de-niros-best-to-worst-movies

http://www.imdb.com/title/tt0075314

http://www.imdb.com/title/tt0970866/awards

http://latinamericanhistory.about.com/od/thevoyagesofcolumbus/tp/Ten-Facts-About-Christopher-Columbus.htm

http://writerschasm.blogspot.com/2010/12/rejection-throughout-history.html

http://www.history.com/news/10-things-you-may-not-know-about-christopher-columbus

http://www.softschools.com/facts/holidays/columbus_day_facts/152

http://www.biography.com/people/christopher-columbus-9254209#synopsis

http://www.findingdulcinea.com/news/on-this-day/May-June-08/On-this-Day--Muhammad-Ali-Convicted-of-Draft-Evasion.html

http://www.theguardian.com/theguardian/2013/apr/29/muhammad-ali-refuses-to-fight-in-vietnam-war-1967

http://pablo-picasso.paintings.name/biography

http://www.biography.com/people/pablo-picasso-9440021#early-life-and-education&awesm=~oEZ2gFbTgjWkVq

http://www.neatorama.com/2008/10/25/10-fun-facts-about-pablo-picasso

http://www.onelifesuccess.net/steven-spielberg-the-man-behind-the-big-screen-life-lessons

http://www.imdb.com/name/nm0000229

http://www.theguardian.com/commentisfree/2012/feb/19/history-of-tanning

http://www.glamour.com/fashion/blogs/dressed/2009/09/5-things-you-can-
thank-coco-ch.html

http://www.oprah.com/style/5-Ways-Coco-Chanel-Has-Inspired-Fashion-Today

http://www.biography.com/people/coco-chanel-9244165#synopsis

http://www.lifetimetv.co.uk/biography/biography-coco-chanel

http://stylecaster.com/breton-stripe

http://www.slideshare.net/bahaarzamindar/coco-chanel-26870736

www.ingramcontent.com/pod-product-compliance
Lightning Source LLC
Chambersburg PA
CBHW051413090426
42737CB00014B/2652